SING
WITH THE BAND

30 POPULAR SONGS FOR MALE SINGERS

ISBN 978-1-61774-129-6

HAL•LEONARD®
CORPORATION

7777 W. BLUEMOUND RD. P.O. BOX 13819 MILWAUKEE, WI 53213

Visit Hal Leonard Online at
www.halleonard.com

VOCAL WARM-UP EXERCISES

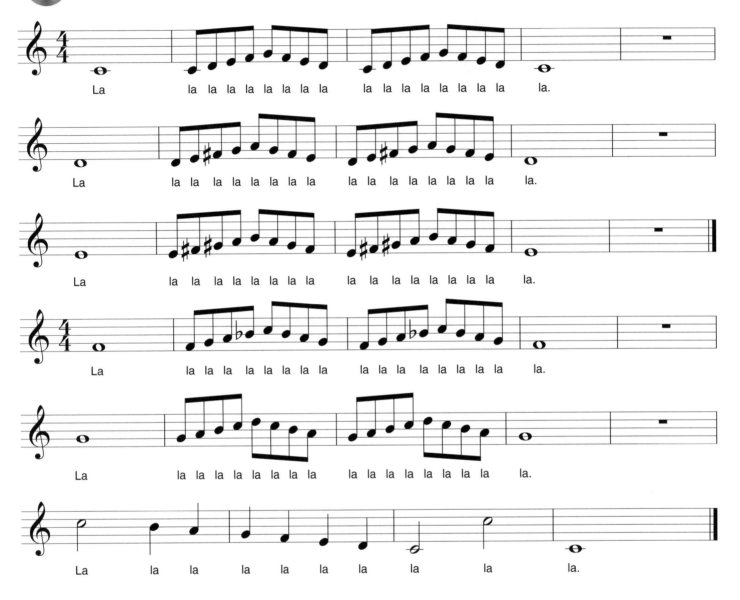

Blue Suede Shoes

Words and Music by Carl Lee Perkins

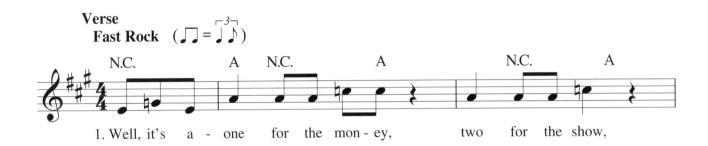

Verse
Fast Rock

1. Well, it's a - one for the mon - ey, two for the show,

three to get read - y, now go, cat, go, but don't ___ you

step on my blue ___ suede shoes. ___ Well, you can

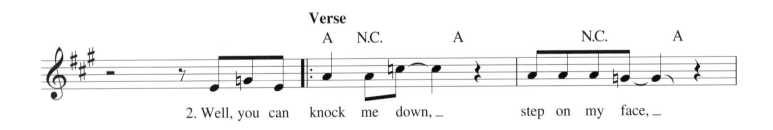

do an - y - thing, ___ but lay off of my blue suede shoes.

Verse

2. Well, you can knock me down, ___ step on my face, ___

slan - der my name all o - ver the place. ___ I'll do an - y - thing ___ that you

Verse

one for the mon-ey, two for the show, three to get read-y, now

go, go, go, but don't ___ you step on my blue ___ suede shoes. ___

___ Well, you can do an-y-thing, ___ but lay off ___

___ of my blue suede shoes. I said a-

Outro

- blue, blue, blue ___ suede shoes. ___ Blue, blue, blue ___

___ suede shoes. ___ Yeah! Blue, blue, blue ___ suede shoes, ___ ba-by.

Blue, blue, blue ___ suede shoes. ___ A-you can do an-y-thing, ___ but lay off ___

___ of my blue suede shoes.

Copacabana
(At the Copa)

Music by Barry Manilow
Lyric by Bruce Sussman and Jack Feldman

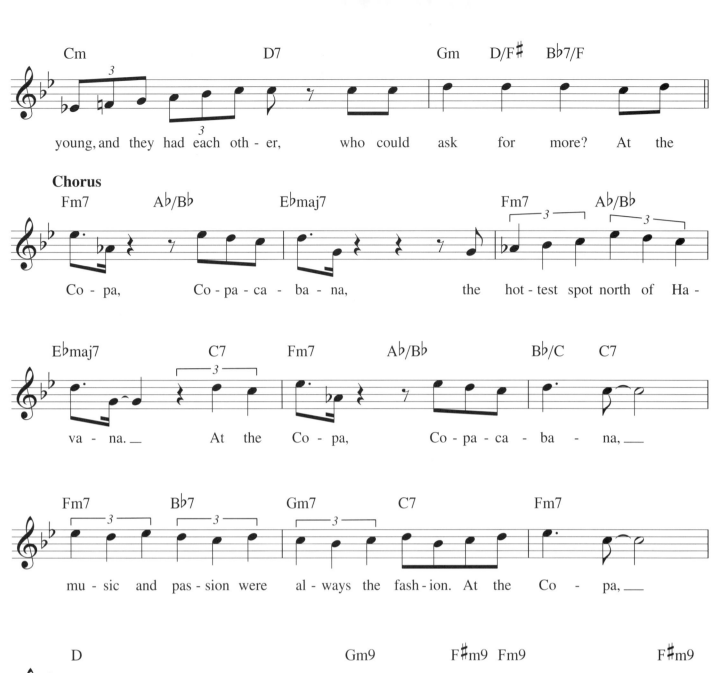

Chorus

Verse

Lo - la danc - ing there.__ And when she fin - ished, he called her

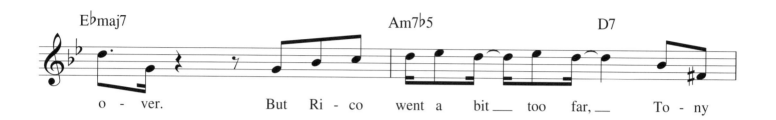

o - ver. But Ri - co went a bit__ too far,__ To - ny

sailed a - cross__ the bar.__ And then the punch - es __ flew, and chairs were

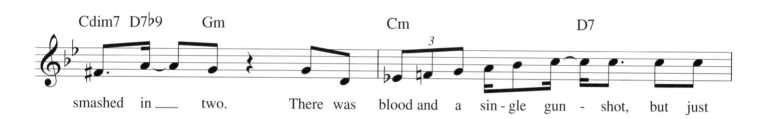

smashed in __ two. There was blood and a sin - gle gun - shot, but just

Chorus

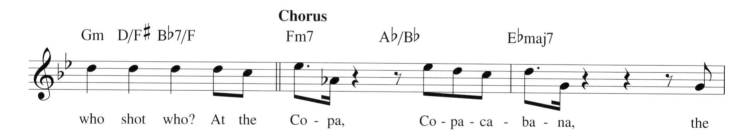

who shot who? At the Co - pa, Co - pa - ca - ba - na, the

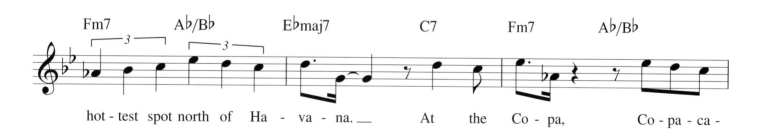

hot - test spot north of Ha - va - na. __ At the Co - pa, Co - pa - ca -

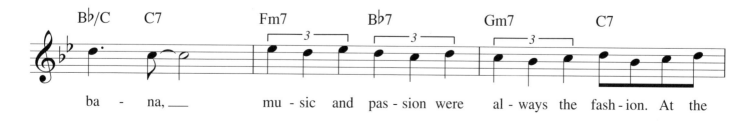

ba - na, __ mu - sic and pas - sion were al - ways the fash - ion. At the

Brick House

**Words and Music by Lionel Richie, Ronald LaPread, Walter Orange,
Milan Williams, Thomas McClary and William King**

Intro
Moderate Funk

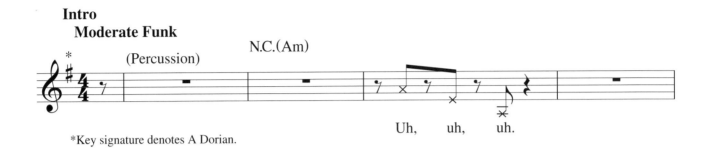

*Key signature denotes A Dorian.

Uh, uh, uh.

Uh.   Woo, _____ wee! _____   Ow, she's a

Chorus

brick   house. _____   She's might-y, might - y, _____ a just

let - tin' it all _____ hang out. _____ She's a brick   house, _____

_____   and that la - dy's stacked _____ and that's a fact. _____

Ain't hold - in' noth - in' back. _____ Ow, she's a brick   house. _____

Well, we're to-geth - er ev -'ry-bod - y knows___ and
Well, ___ she's the one, ___ the on - ly one ___

To Coda ⊕
Verse

this is how the sto - ry goes. ___ 1. You know she's got ev -'ry - thing ___
built like an Am - a - zon. ___

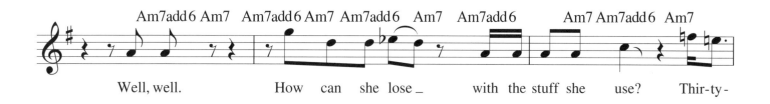

___ that a wom-an needs ___ to get her man.

Well, well. How can she lose ___ with the stuff she use? Thir-ty-

D.S. al Coda

six, twen-ty - four, ___ thir-ty - six. ___ What a win-ning hand. ___ 'Cause she's a

⊕ **Coda**
Verse

2. The clothes she wear ___ has a sex - y way. ___ Makes this

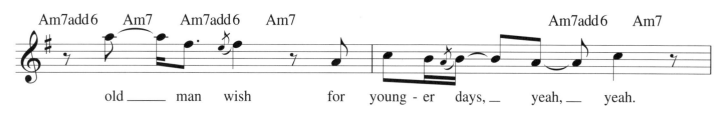

old ___ man wish for young - er days, ___ yeah, ___ yeah.

Da Ya Think I'm Sexy

Words and Music by Rod Stewart and Carmine Appice

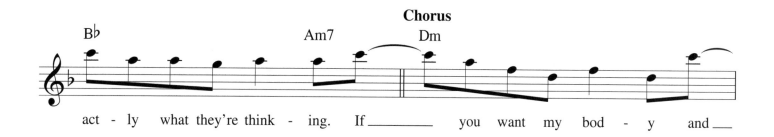

Chorus

act - ly what they're think - ing. If _____ you want my bod - y and _____

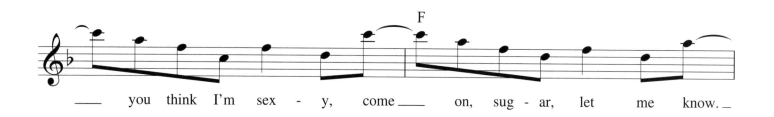

_____ you think I'm sex - y, come _____ on, sug - ar, let me know. _____

_____ If _____ you real - ly need me just _____ reach out and touch me. Come _____

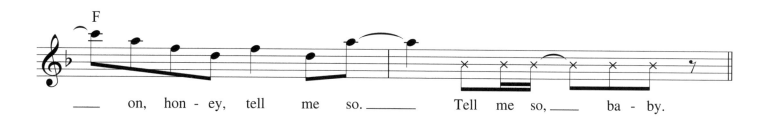

_____ on, hon - ey, tell me so. _____ Tell me so, _____ ba - by.

Interlude

Verse

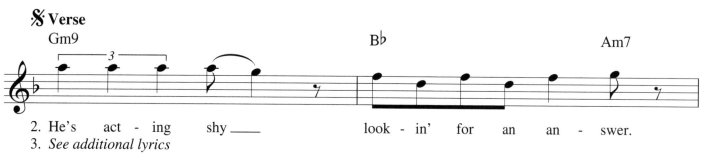

2. He's act - ing shy _____ look - in' for an an - swer.
3. *See additional lyrics*

Come on, ___ hon-ey, let's spend the night to-geth-er. Now

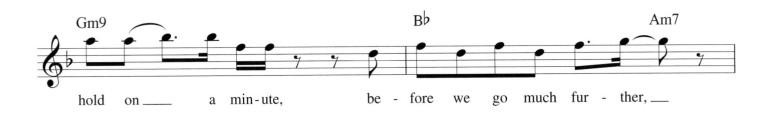

hold on ___ a min-ute, be-fore we go much fur-ther, ___

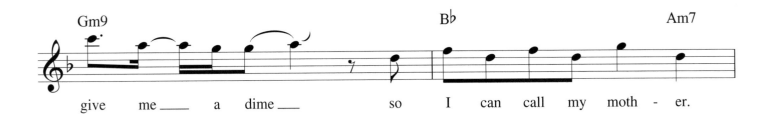

give me ___ a dime ___ so I can call my moth-er.

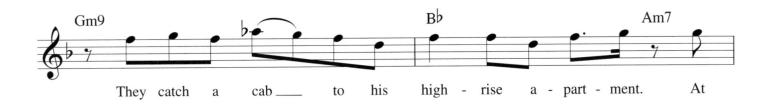

They catch a cab ___ to his high-rise a-part-ment. At

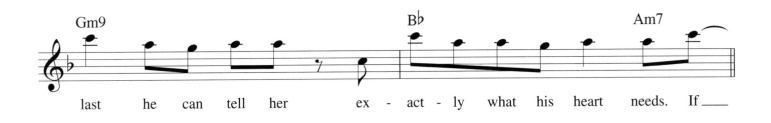

last he can tell her ex-act-ly what his heart needs. If ___

Chorus

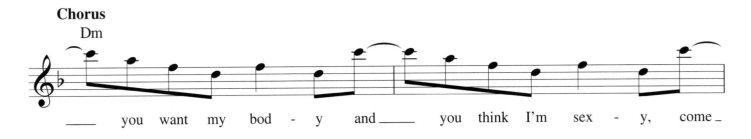

___ you want my bod-y and ___ you think I'm sex-y, come ___

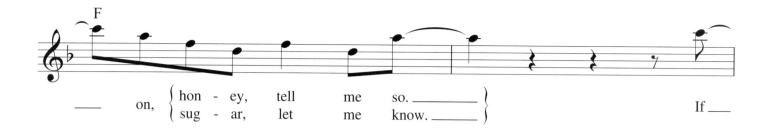

F

___ on, { hon - ey, tell me so. _____
      { sug - ar, let me know. _____   If ___

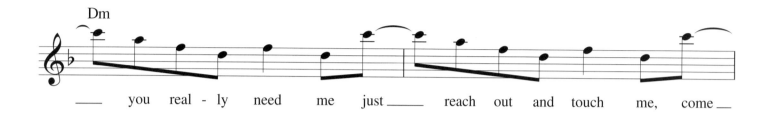

Dm

___ you real - ly need me just ___ reach out and touch me, come ___

To Coda ⊕

F

___ on, { sug - ar, let me know. ___
       { hon - ey, tell me so. ___   Ow! _____

|1. |2.

Interlude

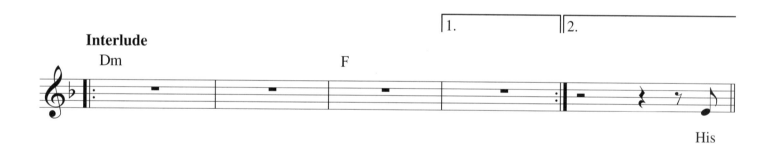

Dm   F

                                                                    His

Bridge

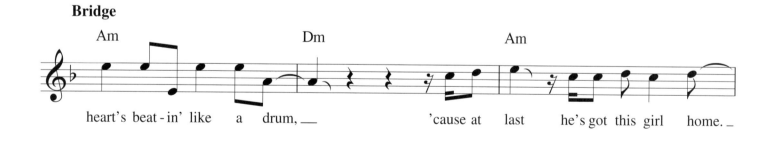

Am   Dm   Am

heart's beat - in' like a drum, ___   'cause at last he's got this girl home. _

Dm   Gm   B♭m

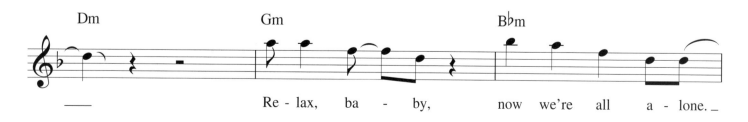

___   Re - lax, ba - by,   now we're all a - lone. _

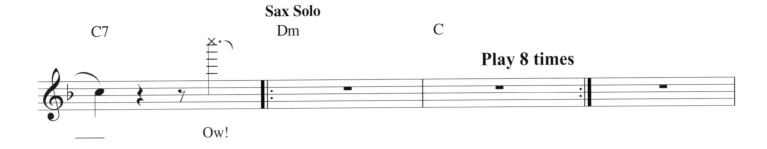

Ow!

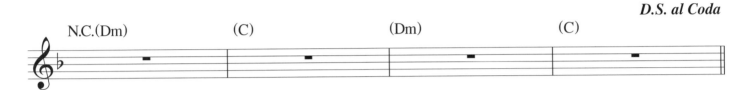

D.S. al Coda

Oo. _____

Sug - ar. __

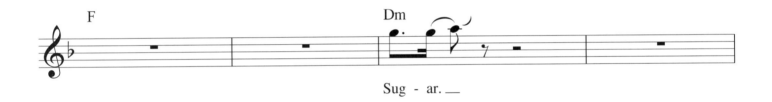

w/ Voc. ad lib., till fade

If you real - ly need me,

Repeat and fade

just reach out and touch me. Come on, sug - ar, let __ me know. _____

Additional Lyrics

3. They wake at dawn, 'cause all the birds are singing.
Two total strangers, but that ain't what they're thinking.
Outside it's cold, misty and it's raining.
They got each other. Neither one's complaining.
He says, "I'm sorry, but I'm out of milk and coffee."
"Never mind, sugar, we can watch the early movie."

Happy Together

Words and Music by Garry Bonner and Alan Gordon

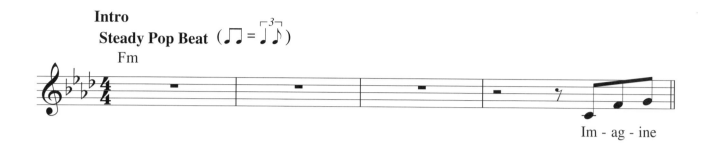

Intro
Steady Pop Beat

Im - ag - ine

Verse

me and you, I do. I think a - bout you day and night. It's on - ly

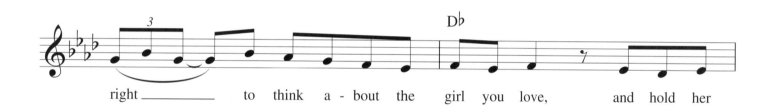

right _____ to think a - bout the girl you love, and hold her

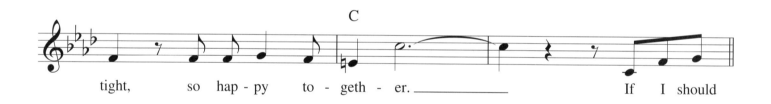

tight, so hap - py to - geth - er. _____ If I should

Verse

call you up, in - vest a dime, and you say you be - long to me, and ease my

mind. Im - ag - ine how the world could be, so ver - y fine, so hap - py to -

Every Breath You Take

Music and Lyrics by Sting

Intro
Moderate Rock

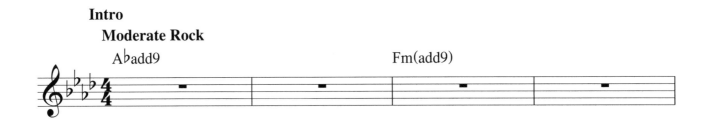

1. Ev -'ry breath   you ___

Verse

___ take,   and ev -'ry move   you ___ make.

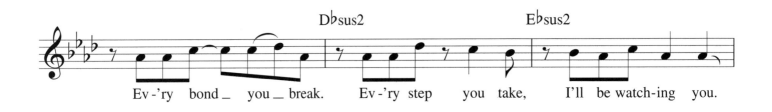

Ev -'ry bond ___ you ___ break.   Ev -'ry step   you take,   I'll be watch-ing   you.

Verse

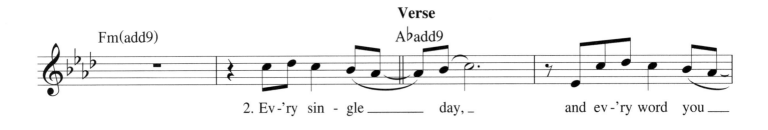

2. Ev -'ry sin - gle _____ day, _   and ev -'ry word   you ___

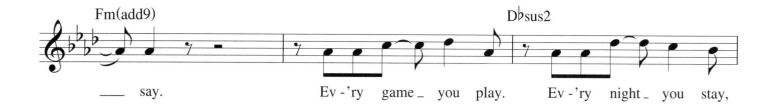

Fm(add9) / Dbsus2

___ say. Ev -'ry game ___ you play. Ev -'ry night ___ you stay,

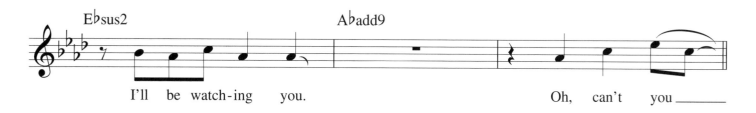

Ebsus2 / Abadd9

I'll be watch-ing you. Oh, can't you ___

𝄋 Bridge

Dbsus2 / Cbsus2 / Abadd9

___ see? ___ You be - long to ___ me. ___

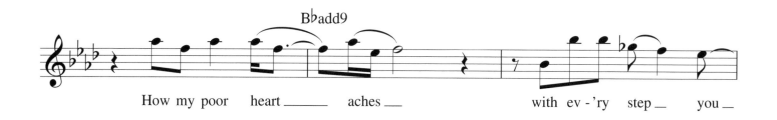

Bbadd9

How my poor heart ___ aches ___ with ev -'ry step ___ you ___

Verse

Ebsus2 / Abadd9

___ take. 3., 4. Ev -'ry move you ___ make,

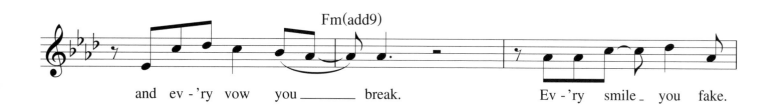

Fm(add9)

and ev -'ry vow you ___ break. Ev -'ry smile ___ you fake.

To Coda ⊕

Dbsus2 / Ebsus2 / Fm(add9)

Ev -'ry claim ___ you stake, I'll be watch-ing you.

Bridge

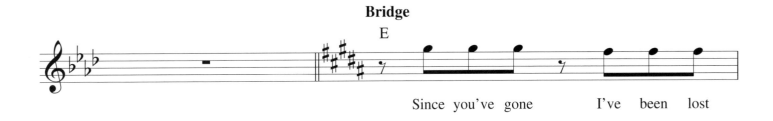

Since you've gone   I've been lost

with - out ___ a   trace,   I dream at night I can on -

- ly   see ___ your   face.   I look a - round, but it's

you   I   can't ___   re - place.   I feel so cold   and   I

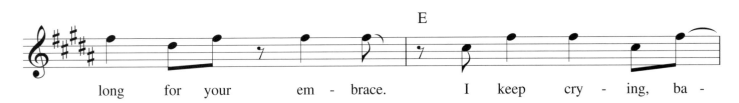

long   for your   em - brace.   I keep   cry - ing,   ba -

Interlude

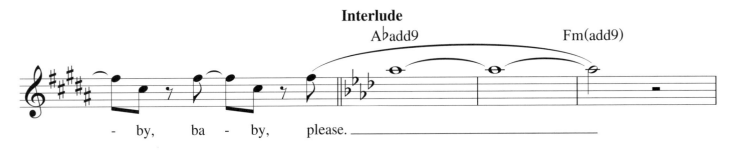

- by,   ba - by,   please. ___

Oh, can't you _____

⊕ Coda

Ev - 'ry move __ you make. Ev - 'ry step you take,

I'll be watch-ing you.

Outro
w/ Voc. ad lib., till fade

I'll be watch - ing _____ you.

1., 5. (Ev -'ry breath __ you take. Ev -'ry move __ you make.
2., 4., 6. (Ev -'ry sin - gle day. Ev -'ry word __ you say.
3. (Ev -'ry move __ you make. Ev -'ry vow __ you break.

Play 5 times & fade

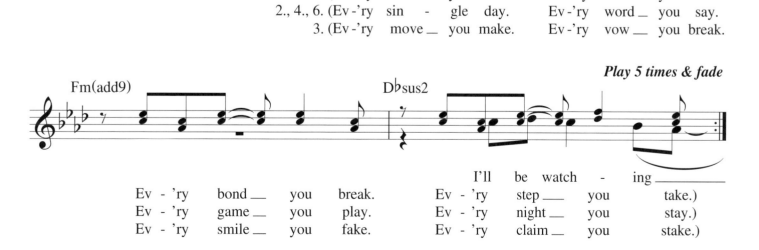

I'll be watch - ing _____

Ev - 'ry bond __ you break. Ev - 'ry step ___ you take.)
Ev - 'ry game __ you play. Ev - 'ry night __ you stay.)
Ev - 'ry smile __ you fake. Ev - 'ry claim __ you stake.)

Georgia On My Mind

Words by Stuart Gorrell
Music by Hoagy Carmichael

Intro
Ballad

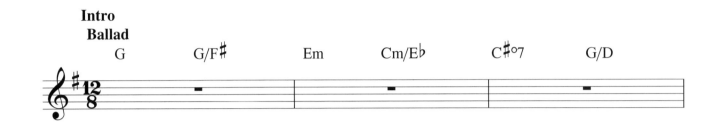

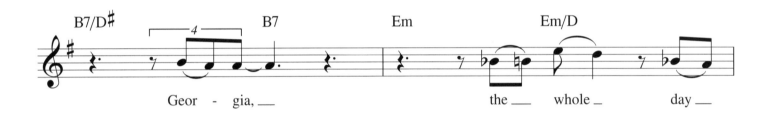

Verse

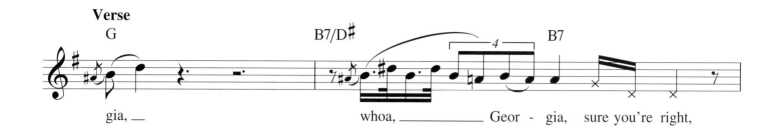

gia, __ whoa, _____ Geor - gia, sure you're right,

no __ peace, __ no peace I find. ___ Just an

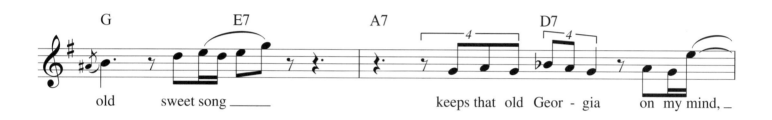

old sweet song _____ keeps that old Geor - gia on my mind, __

_____ whoa, _____ I said, just an

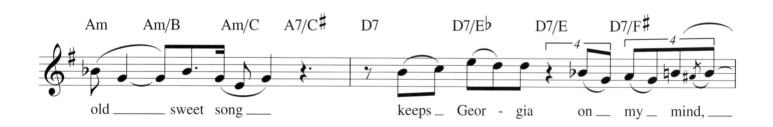

old _____ sweet song ___ keeps _ Geor - gia on _ my _ mind, ___

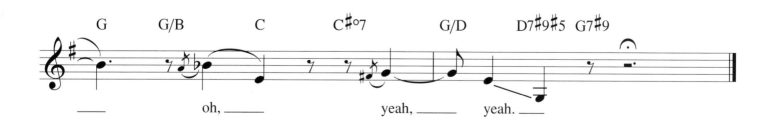

___ oh, _____ yeah, _____ yeah. ___

Hello

Words and Music by Lionel Richie

Intro

Pop Ballad

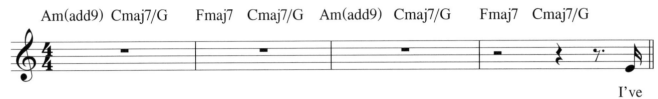

I've

Verse

been a-lone _ with you _ in-side _ my _____ mind; _____ and

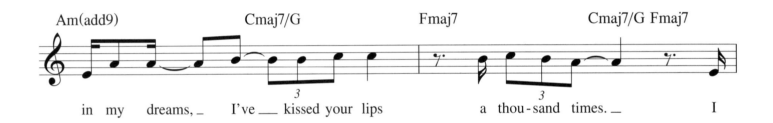

in my dreams, _ I've ___ kissed your lips a thou-sand times. _ I

some-times _____ see you pass out-side _ my _____ door. _____ Hel-

lo. _ Is it me you're _ look-in' ____ for? ____ I

Chorus

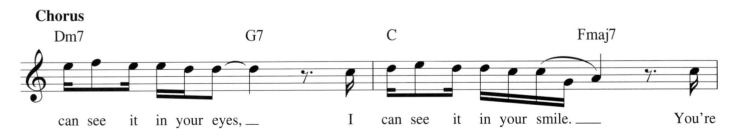

can see it in your eyes, _ I can see it in your smile. _ You're

B♭   E7/G♯   Am   E7/B   Am/C   E7/B

all I ev - er want - ed,   and my arms are o - pen wide. _   'Cause you

Dm7   G7   C   Fmaj7

know   just what to say   and you know just what to do, _____   and I

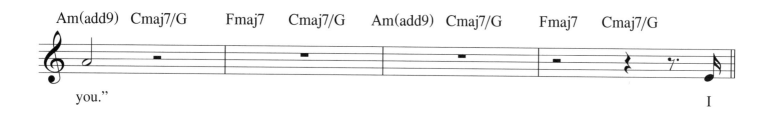

B♭   Am/E   E7

want   to tell ___ you so _____ much, ___   "I love

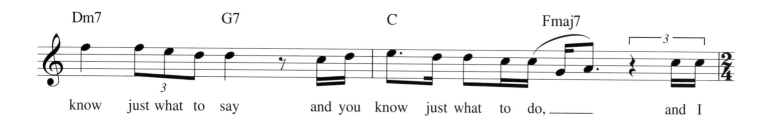

Am(add9) Cmaj7/G   Fmaj7   Cmaj7/G   Am(add9) Cmaj7/G   Fmaj7   Cmaj7/G

you."   I

Verse

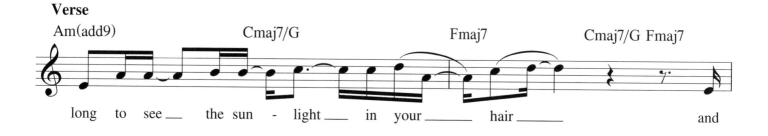

Am(add9)   Cmaj7/G   Fmaj7   Cmaj7/G Fmaj7

long   to see ___ the sun - light ___ in your _____ hair _____   and

Am(add9)   Cmaj7/G   Fmaj7   Cmaj7/G Fmaj7

tell   you time _ and time _ a - gain _   how much _ I care. _   Some-

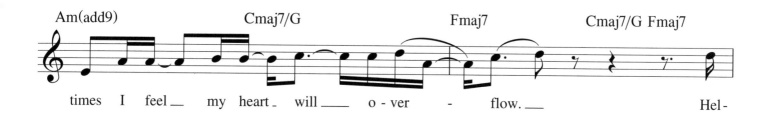

Am(add9)   Cmaj7/G   Fmaj7   Cmaj7/G Fmaj7

times I feel ___ my heart _ will ___ o - ver - flow. ___   Hel-

lo. ____ I've just got to let you know._____ 'Cause I

Chorus

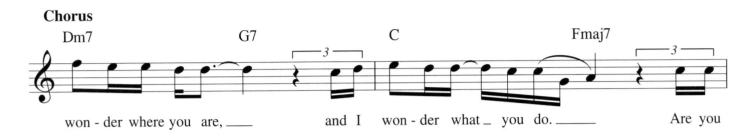

won - der where you are, ____ and I won - der what _ you do. _____ Are you

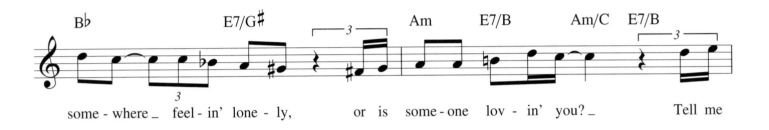

some - where _ feel - in' lone - ly, or is some - one lov - in' you? _ Tell me

how to win your heart, _ for I have - n't got __ a clue. ____ But

let me start _ by say - in', "I love you."

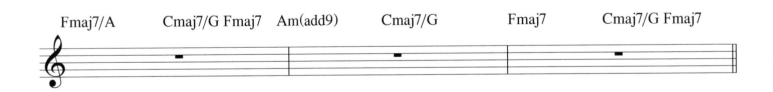

Interlude

34

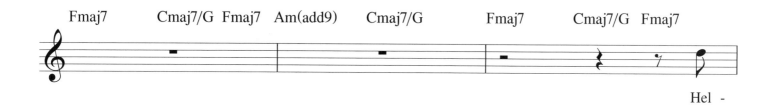

Hel -

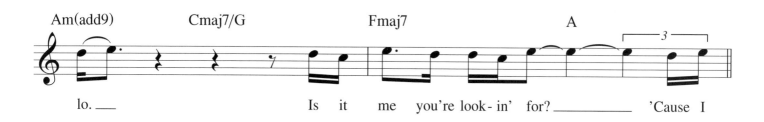

lo. ___   Is it me you're look - in' for? _____ 'Cause I

Chorus

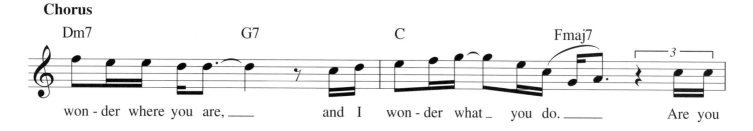

won - der where you are, ___   and I won - der what _ you do. _____   Are you

some - where feel - in' lone - ly,   or is some - one lov - ing you? _   Tell

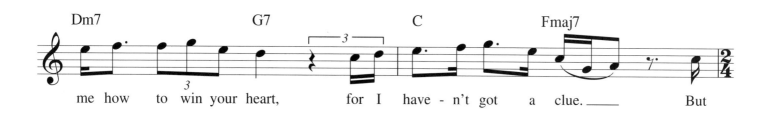

me how to win your heart,   for I have - n't got a clue. ___   But

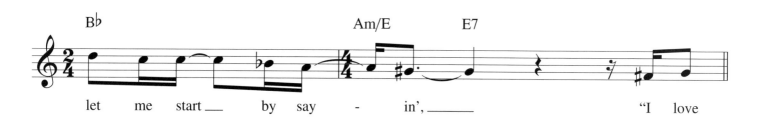

let me start ___ by say - in', _____   "I love

Outro

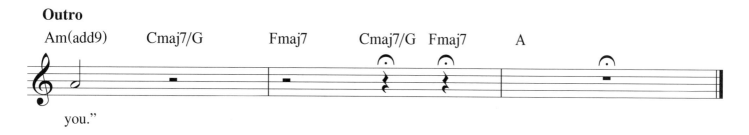

you."

Hey, Good Lookin'

Words and Music by Hank Williams

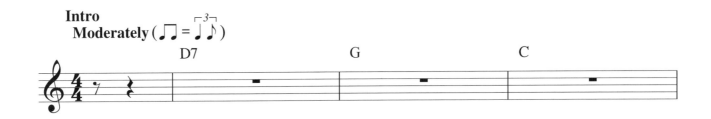

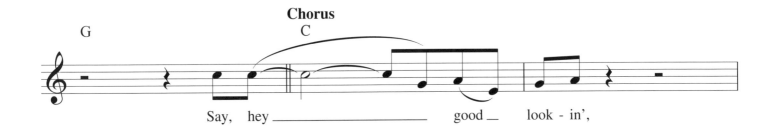

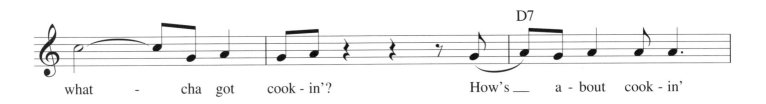

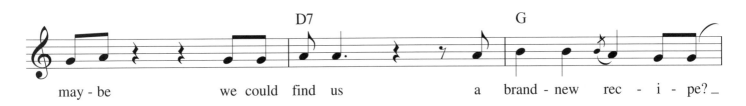

—

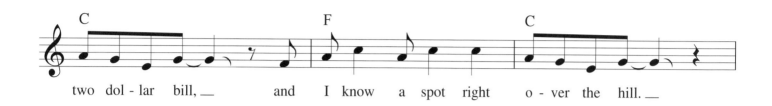

I got a hot rod Ford and a

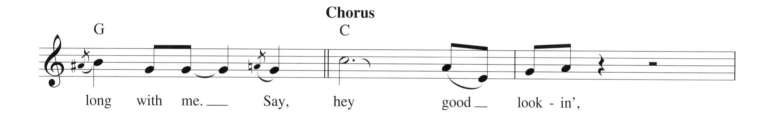

two dol - lar bill, __ and I know a spot right o - ver the hill. __

There's so - da pop and the danc - in' is free, __ so if you wan - na have fun come a-

Chorus

long with me. __ Say, hey good __ look - in',

what - cha got cook - in'? How's __ a - bout cook - in'

some - thin' up ____ with me? _____

Interlude

28

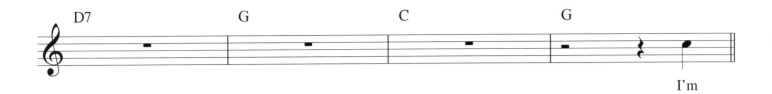

I'm

Chorus

free _____ and __ read - y   so we _____ can go __

stead - y.   How's __ a - bout sav - in'   all your time __ for me? __

Verse

__   2. No   more

look - in',   I know _____ I been __ took - en.   How's _

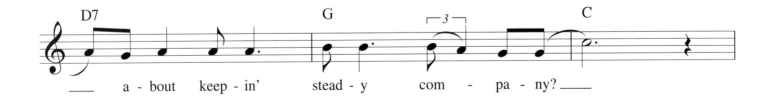

___ a - bout keep - in'   stead - y   com - pa - ny? _____

I'm gon - na throw my date book o - ver the fence, ___ and

find me ___ one for five or ten cents, ___ and keep it 'til _____ it's

cov - ered with age ___ 'cause I'm a - writ - in' your name ___ down on ev - 'ry page. ___ Say,

Outro-Chorus

hey good ___ look - in', what - cha got

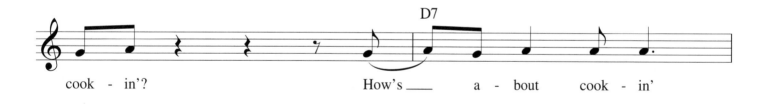

cook - in'? How's ___ a - bout cook - in'

some - thin' up ___ with me? _____

Hey Jude

Words and Music by John Lennon and Paul McCartney

The move - ment you need _____ is on _____ your shoul -

- der. _____ Na, na, na, na, _____ na, na, na, na, na. _____ Yeah. _

Verse

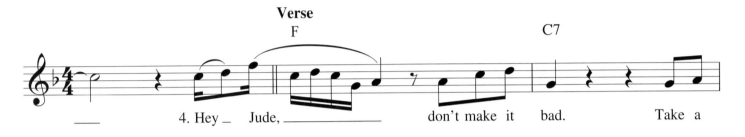

_____ 4. Hey _ Jude, _____ don't make it bad. Take a

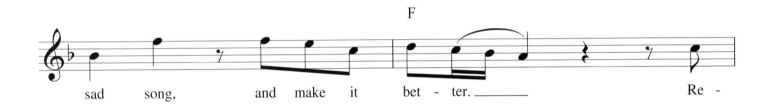

sad song, and make it bet - ter. _____ Re -

mem - ber to let her un - der your skin. Then you be - gin __

_____ to make it bet - ter, bet - ter, bet - ter, bet - ter, bet - ter, bet - ter, oh.

Outro *Repeat and fade*

Na, na, na, na, na, na, na. Na, na, na, na. Hey _ Jude. _

How Sweet It Is
(To Be Loved by You)

Words and Music by Edward Holland, Lamont Dozier and Brian Holland

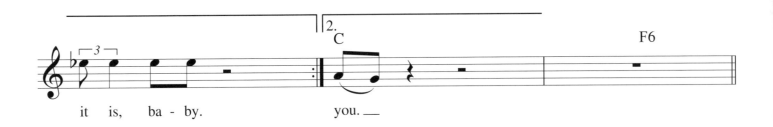

it is, ba - by. you. ___

Interlude

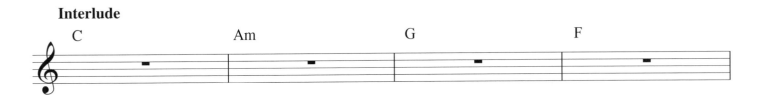

You were bet - ter to me ___ than I've ___ been to my - self. ___

For me there's ___ you, ___ and no - bod - y else. I wan - na stop ___

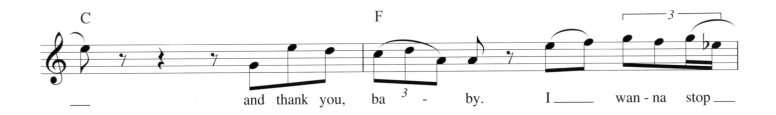

___ and thank you, ba - by. I ___ wan - na stop ___

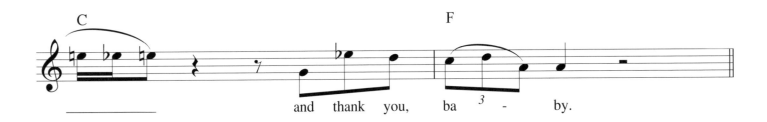

___ and thank you, ba - by.

Chorus

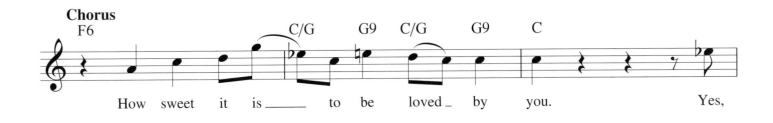

How sweet it is ___ to be loved ___ by you. Yes,

it is, _____ ba - by. _____ How sweet it is _____

_____ to be _____ loved _ by you. _____

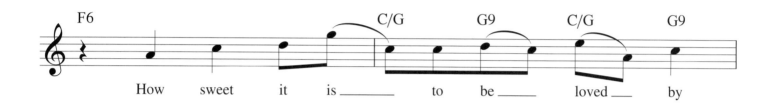

How sweet it is _____ to be _____ loved _____ by

you. _____ Yes, it is, ba - by. _____

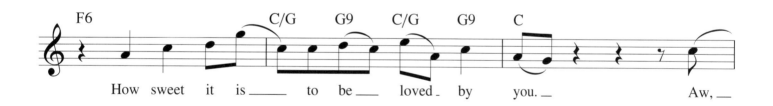

How sweet it is _____ to be _____ loved _ by you. _____ Aw, _____

_____ ba - by. How sweet it is _____ to be _____ loved _ by

you. _____ Yes, it is, ba - by. _____

Home

Words and Music by Amy Foster-Gillies, Michael Bublé and Alan Chang

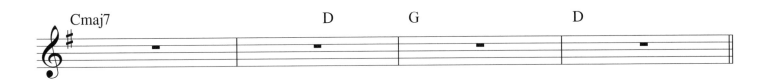

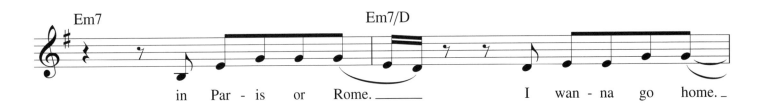

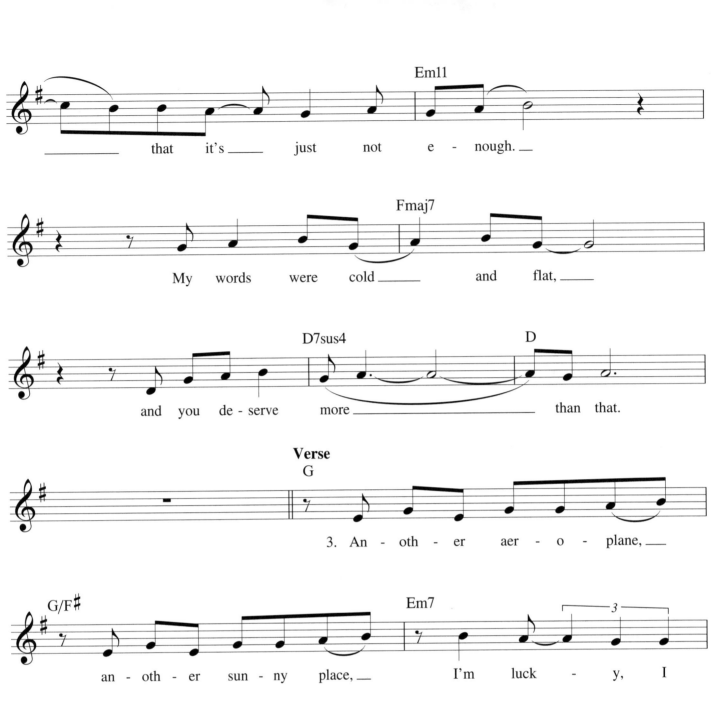

that it's ___ just not e - nough. ___

My words were cold ___ and flat, ___

and you de - serve more ___ than that.

Verse

3. An - oth - er aer - o - plane, ___

an - oth - er sun - ny place, ___ I'm luck - y, I

know, ___ but I wan - na go home, ___

mmm, I've got to go home. Let me go home. ___

Chorus

Interlude

Bridge

that this was not your dream, but you al - ways be -

lieved in me.

Verse

4. An - oth - er win - ter day has come and gone a - way

in ei - ther Par - is or Rome, and I wan - na go home.

Let me go home.

Verse

5. And I'm sur - round - ed by

a mil - lion peo - ple, I, I still feel a - lone,

and let me go home.

Chorus-Outro

Freely

How Deep Is Your Love

from the Motion Picture SATURDAY NIGHT FEVER

Words and Music by Barry Gibb, Robin Gibb and Maurice Gibb

Intro
Moderately

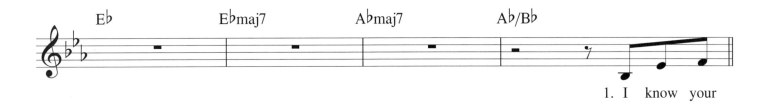

Verse

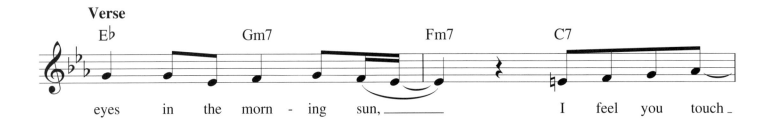

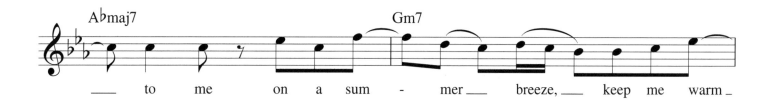

_____ to me on a sum - mer _____ breeze, _____ keep me warm _

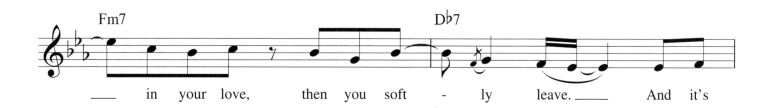

_____ in your love, then you soft - ly leave. _____ And it's

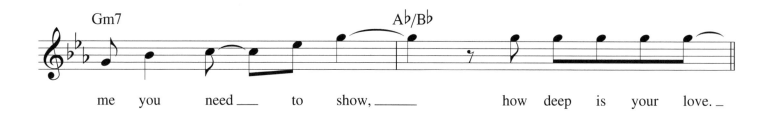

me you need _____ to show, _____ how deep is your love. _

Chorus

_____

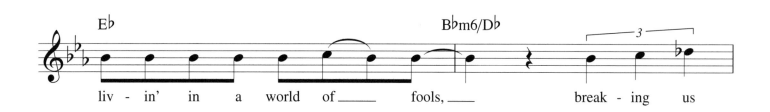

'Cause we're

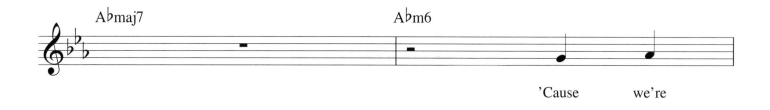

liv - in' in a world of _____ fools, _____ break - ing us

down, when they all _____ should let us be. _____

We be-long _____ to you _____ and _____ me. _____

Verse

_____ 2. I be-lieve in you, _____ you know the door _____

_____ to my ver - y soul. _____ You're the light _____

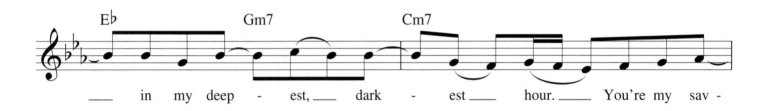

_____ in my deep - est, _____ dark - est _____ hour. _____ You're my sav -

- iour when _____ I'm bored. _____ And you may _____

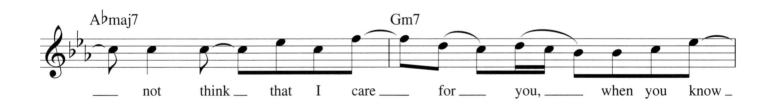

_____ not think _____ that I care _____ for _____ you, _____ when you know _____

_____ down in - side that I real - ly do. _____ Well, it's me _____

56

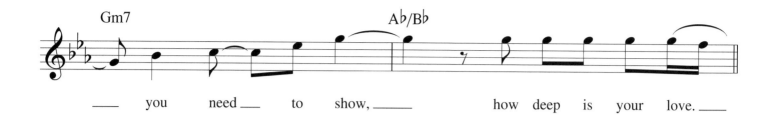

_____ you need _____ to show, _____ how deep is your love. _____

Chorus

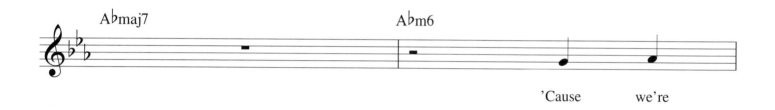

'Cause we're

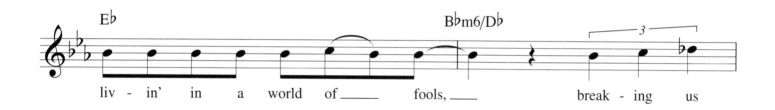

liv - in' in a world of _____ fools, ___ break - ing us

down, when they all _____ should let us be. _____

_____ We be - long _____ to you _____ and _____ me. _____

Verse

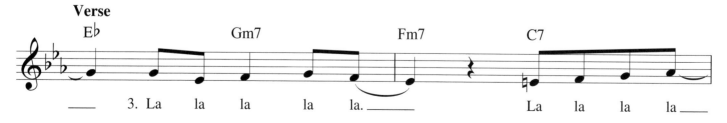

_____ 3. La la la la la. _____ La la la la _____

Fm7　　　　　G7　　　　　Ab/Bb

___ la la la la la. ___ La la la ___

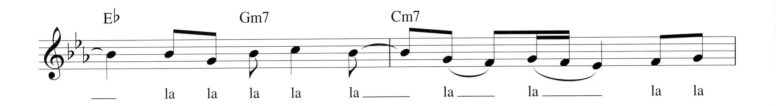

Eb　　　　　Gm7　　　　　Cm7

___ la la la la la ___ la ___ la ___ la la

Fm7　　　　　　　　　Ab/Bb

la la la ___ la ___ la. ___ Then you come _

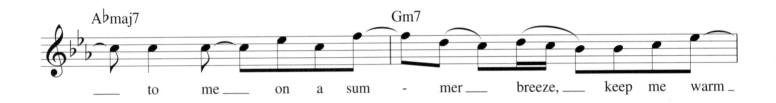

Abmaj7　　　　　　　Gm7

___ to me ___ on a sum - mer ___ breeze, ___ keep me warm _

Fm7　　　　　　　Db7

___ in your love, then you soft - ly leave. ___ And it's

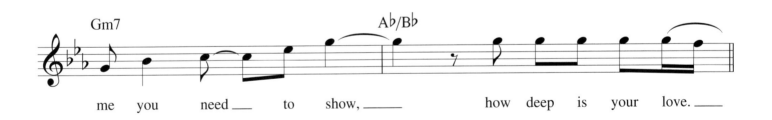

Gm7　　　　　　　Ab/Bb

me you need ___ to show, ___ how deep is your love. ___

Chorus

Eb　　　　　　　　　　Ebmaj7

___

58

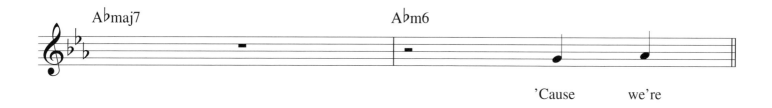

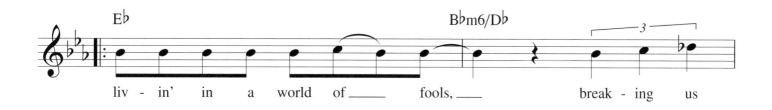

'Cause we're

liv - in' in a world of _____ fools, _____ break - ing us

down, when they all _____ should let us be. _____

We be - long _____ to you _____ and _____ me. _____

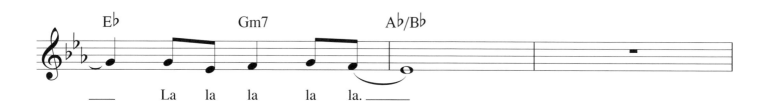

_____ La la la la la. _____

Repeat and Fade

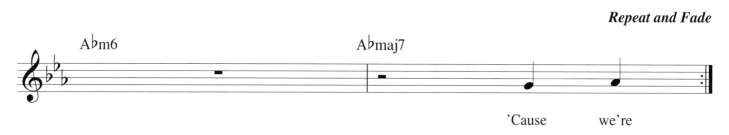

'Cause we're

59

Jessie's Girl

Words and Music by Rick Springfield

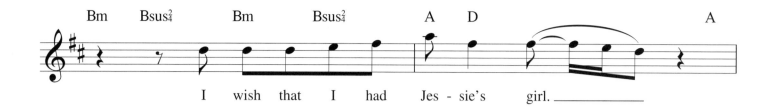

I wish that I had Jes - sie's girl. _____

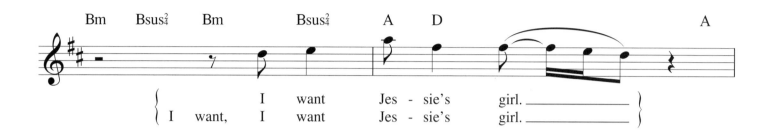

I want Jes - sie's girl. _____
I want, I want Jes - sie's girl. _____

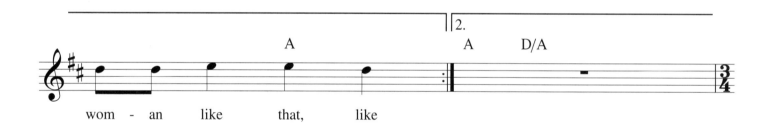

Where can I find a _____

wom - an like that, like

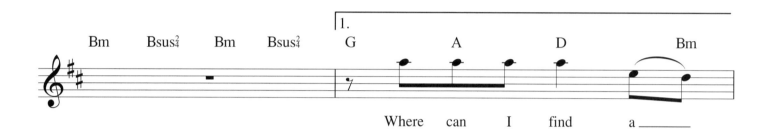

Additional Lyrics

2. I play along with the charade.
   There doesn't seem to be a reason to change.
   You know, I feel so dirty when they start talkin' cute.
   I wanna tell her that I love her, but the point is prob'ly moot.
   'Cause she's watchin' him with those eyes.
   And she's lovin' him with that body, I just know it.
   And he's holding her in his arms late, late at night.

The Lady Is a Tramp

from BABES IN ARMS
from WORDS AND MUSIC
Words by Lorenz Hart
Music by Richard Rodgers

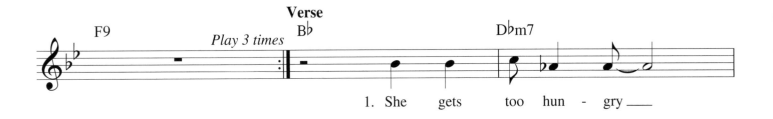

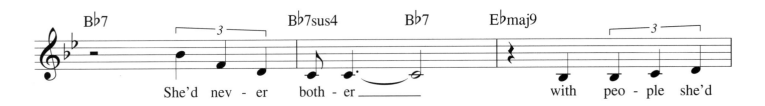

Verse

She's broke, and it's oke. 3. Hates Cal - i - for -

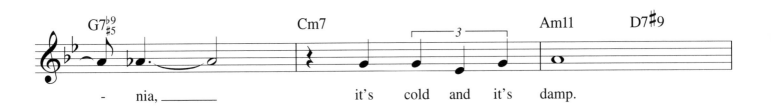

- nia, _____ it's cold and it's damp.

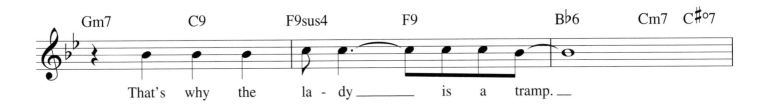

That's why the la - dy _____ is a tramp. _

Verse

4. She _____ gets too _____ hun - gry _____

to wait for din - ner at eight. She loves the thea -

- tre, _____ but nev - er comes late.

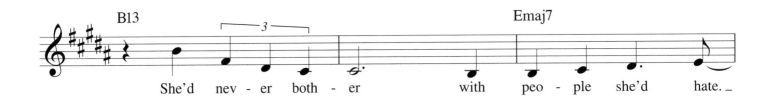

She'd nev - er both - er with peo - ple she'd hate. _

Em9 A13 D#m7 G#7 C#m7 F#9

_____ That's why the la - dy _____ is a tramp. _

B6 G#13#9 C#7#9#5 F#7#9 **Verse** B

_____ 5. She'll _____ have no _____

Dm6 C#m9 *3* F#13 F#7#9#5

_____ crap games _ with sharp - ies or frauds.

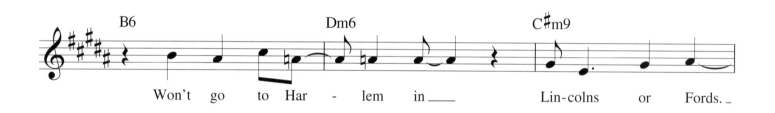

B6 Dm6 C#m9

Won't go to Har - lem in _____ Lin-colns or Fords. _

F#13 B *3* B9

_____ She won't _ dish the dirt with

Emaj9 A9 B6 G#7

the rest of the broads. _____ That's why the

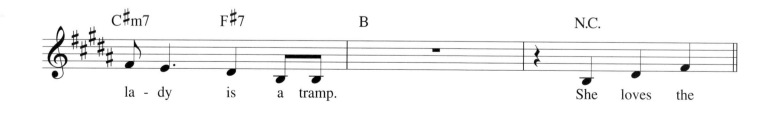

C#m7 F#7 B N.C.

la - dy is a tramp. She loves the

Bridge

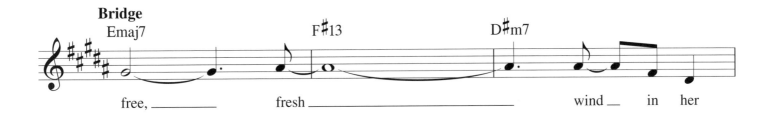

free, _____ fresh _____ wind _ in her

hair, life _____ with - out care.

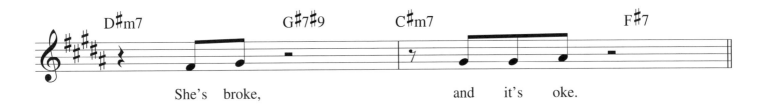

She's broke, and it's oke.

Outro-Verse

Hates Cal - i - for - nia, _____ it's so cold and so

damp. That's why the la - dy, _____

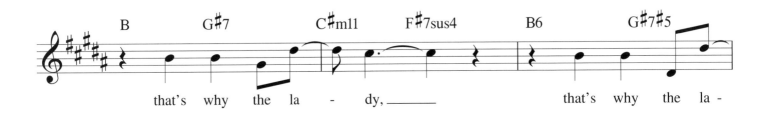

that's why the la - dy, _____ that's why the la -

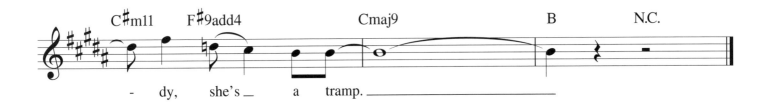

- dy, she's _ a tramp. _____

Smooth

Words by Rob Thomas
Music by Rob Thomas and Itaal Shur

Intro
Moderately

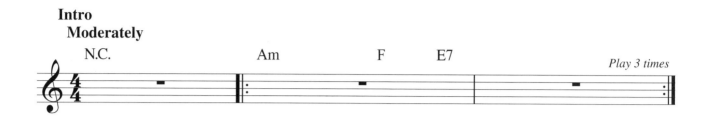

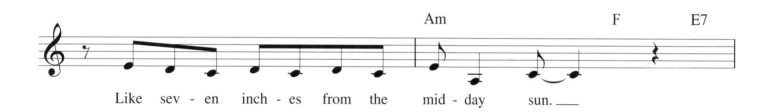

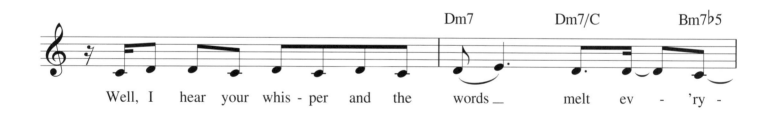

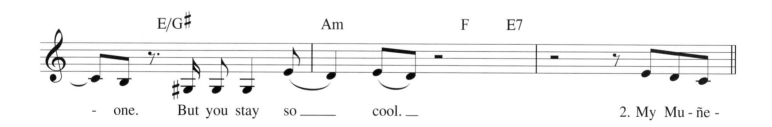

Let's Get It On

Words and Music by Marvin Gaye and Ed Townsend

Bridge

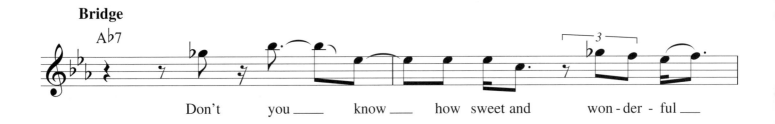

Don't you ___ know ___ how sweet and won-der-ful ___

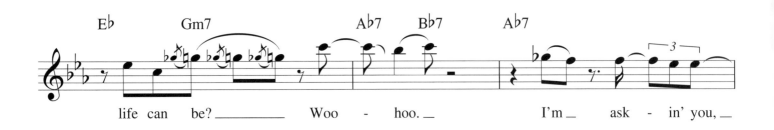

life can be? ___ Woo - hoo. ___ I'm ___ ask - in' you,

___ ba - by, to get it on with me. ___ Oo, ___ oo, ___

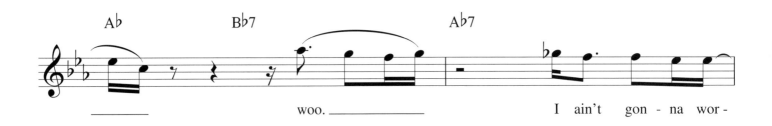

___ woo. ___ I ain't gon - na wor -

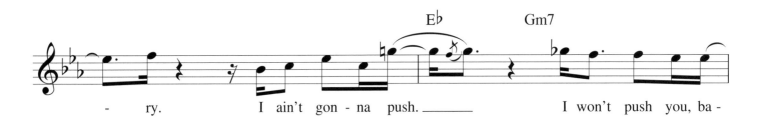

- ry. I ain't gon - na push. ___ I won't push you, ba -

- by. So come on, come on, come on, come on, come on, ba -

- by, stop beat - in' 'round ___ the bush. ___ Hey,

know __ what I've __ been dream - in' of. ___ Don't ya, ba -

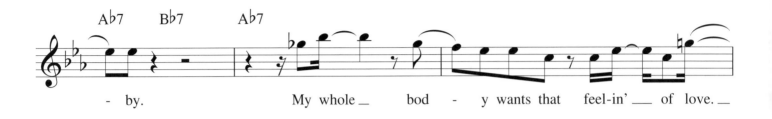

- by. My whole __ bod - y wants that feel-in' __ of love. __

_____ Ah, help me! Whew! __ I ain't gon-na wor - ry. _

_____ No, I ain't gon - na push. _____ I won't push you, ba -

- by. Whew! Come on, come on, come on, come on, come on, dar -

- lin', stop beat-in' 'round the bush. _____

Chorus

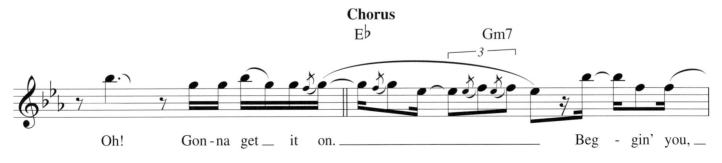

Oh! Gon -na get __ it on. _____ Beg - gin' you, __

My Way

English Words by Paul Anka
Original French Words by Gilles Thibault
Music by Jacques Revaux and Claude Francois

Intro
Moderately slow
Verse

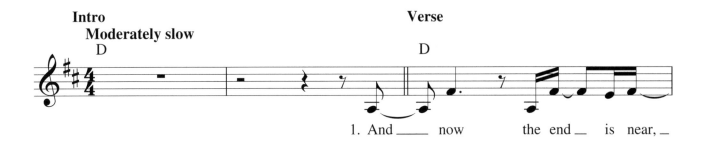

1. And ___ now ___ the end ___ is near, ___

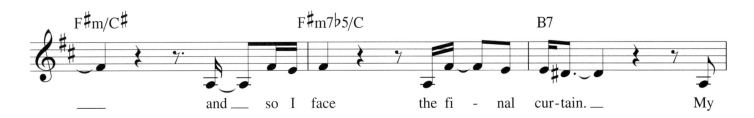

___ and ___ so I face ___ the fi - nal cur - tain. ___ My

friend, ___ I'll say it clear, ___ I'll state my case, ___ of which I'm

cer - tain. ___ I've lived ___ a life that's full ___ I've ___ trav - eled each ___

___ and ev - 'ry high - way, ___ and more, ___ much more than ___

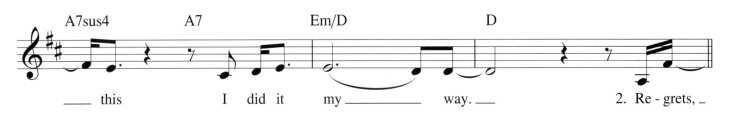

___ this ___ I did it my _____ way. ___ 2. Re - grets, ___

A   A/G   F♯m7   Bm7

___ doubt, ___ I ate it up   and _ spit it out. ___   I faced it all, ___

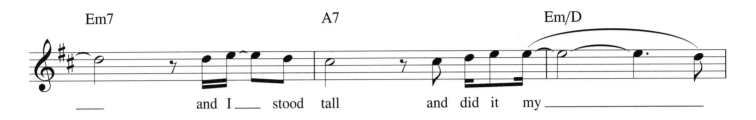

Em7   A7   Em/D

___ and I ___ stood tall   and did it my _____

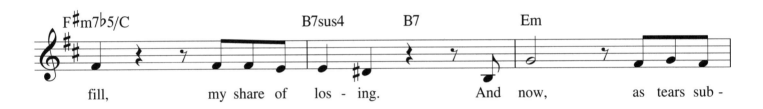

Verse

D   D   F♯m/C♯

way. _____ 3. I've ___ loved, I've laughed and cried. I've had my

F♯m7♭5/C   B7sus4 B7   Em

fill, my share of los - ing. And now, as tears sub -

Em/D   A7/C♯   Em/D   D

side, I find it all ___ so a - mus - ing. To

  Dmaj7   D9sus4 D7♭9   G G+ G6 G+

think I did all that, ___ and may I say, ___ not __ in a

Em7♭5   D/A   A7sus4 A7

shy way, ___ "Oh ___ no, oh no, not me, I ___ did it

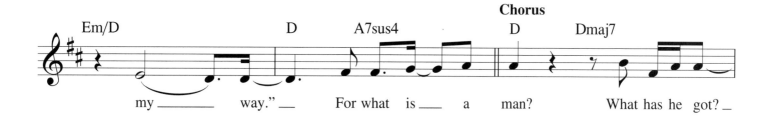

my _____ way." ___ For what is ___ a man? What has he got? ___

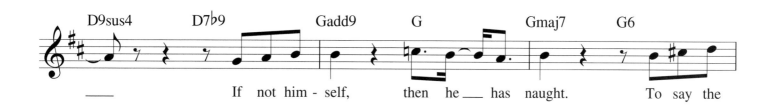

___ If not him - self, then he ___ has naught. To say the

things he tru - ly feels and not the words ___ of one who kneels, ___

___ the re-cord shows ___ I took the blows ___ and did it

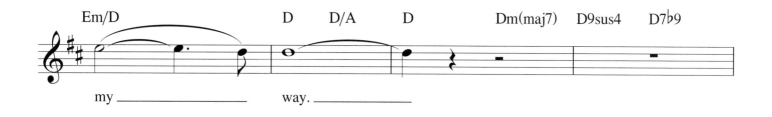

my _____ way. _____

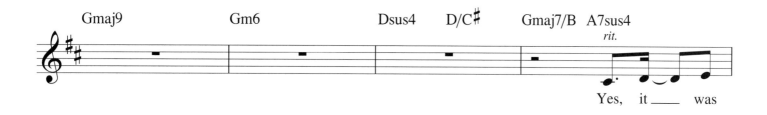

Yes, it ___ was

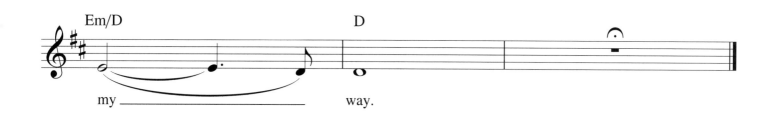

my _____ way.

Route 66

by Bobby Troup

- staff, Ar - i - zo - na, don't ___ for - get Wi - no - na, King -

- man, Bar - stow, San Ber - nar - di - no. Won't ___ you get hip ___

___ to this time - ly tip, ___ when you make that

Cal - i - for - nia trip? ___ Get your kicks ___

___ on Route ___ Six - ty Six. ___ Get your kicks ___

Outro

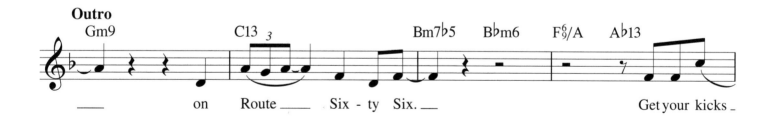

___ on Route ___ Six - ty Six. ___ Get your kicks ___

___ on Route ___ Six - ty Six. ___

Somebody to Love

Words and Music by Freddie Mercury

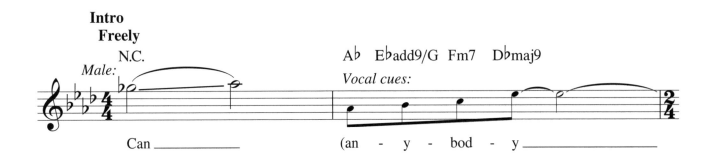

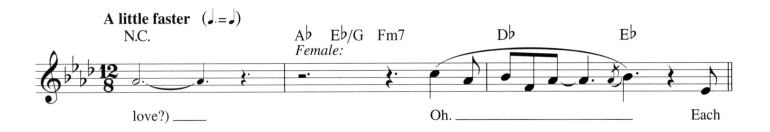

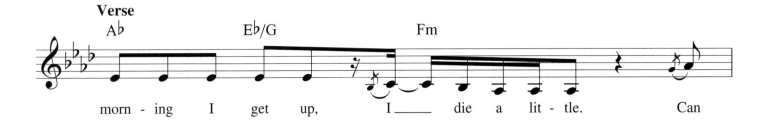

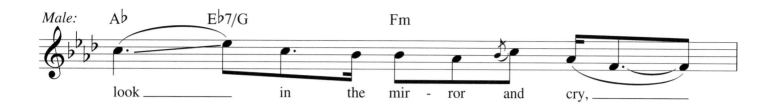

Male: look _____ in the mir - ror and cry, _____

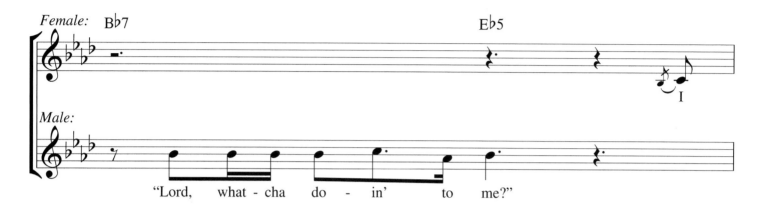

Female: "Lord, what - cha do - in' to me?" I

Male:

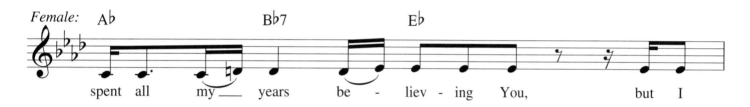

Female: spent all my ___ years be - liev - ing You, but I

just can't get no re - lief, Lord.

Chorus

Female: Can

Male: Some - bod - y, whoa, some - bod - y, _____ can

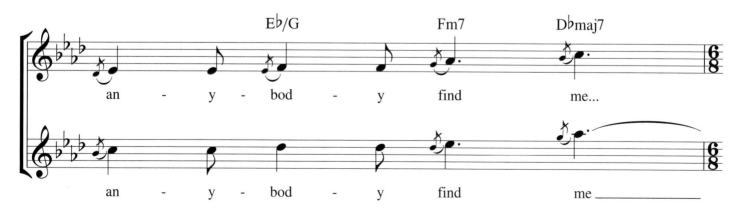

an - y - bod - y find me...

an - y - bod - y find me _____

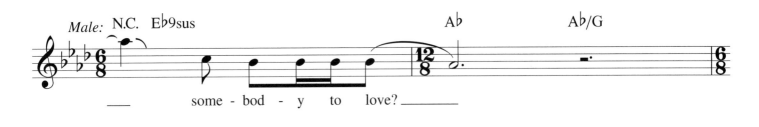

Verse

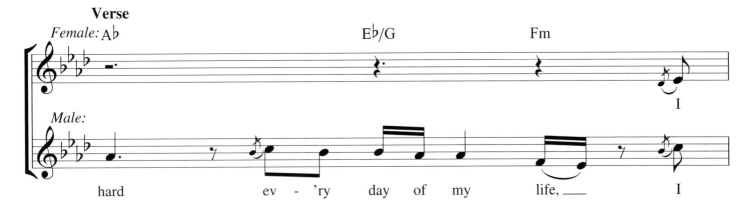

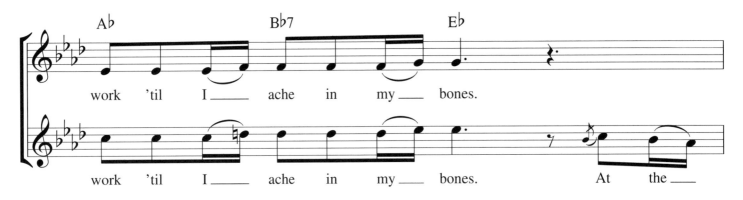

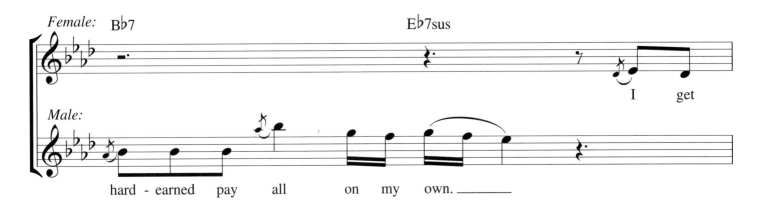

down on my ___ knees and I ___ start to pray 'til the

tears run down from my ___ eyes, Lord.

Chorus

Female: can

Male: Some - bod - y, whoa, some - bod - y, ___ can

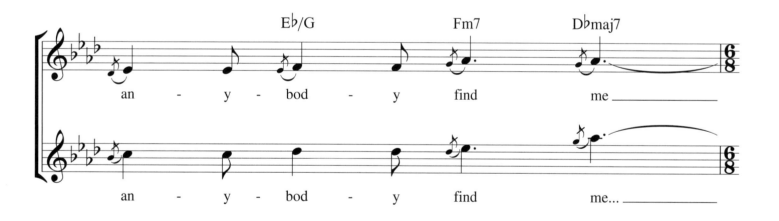

an - y - bod - y find me ___

an - y - bod - y find me... ___

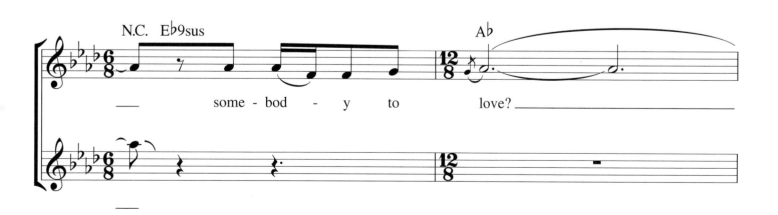

___ some - bod - y to love? ___

Bridge

92

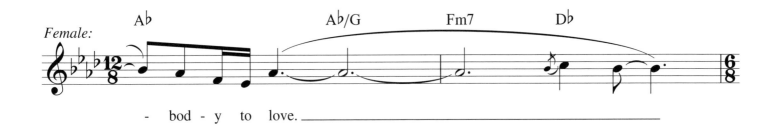

- bod - y to love. _____

Verse

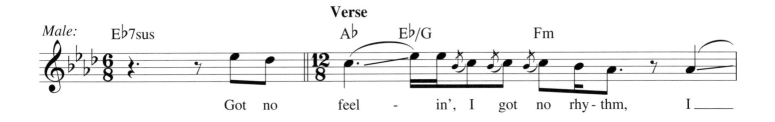

Got no feel - in', I got no rhy - thm, I _____

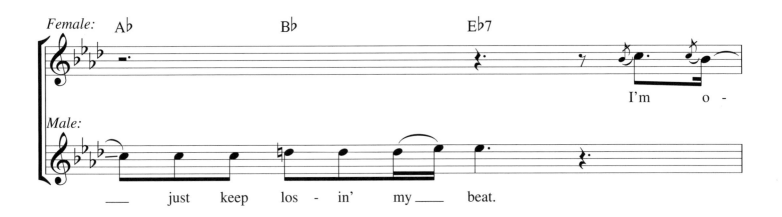

I'm o -

_____ just keep los - in' my _____ beat.

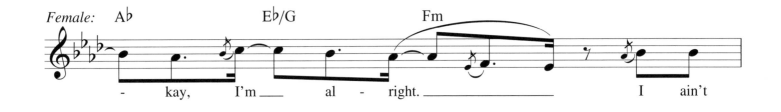

- kay, I'm _____ al - right. _____ I ain't

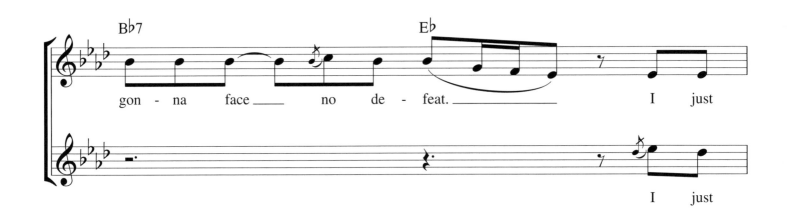

gon - na face _____ no de - feat. _____ I just

I just

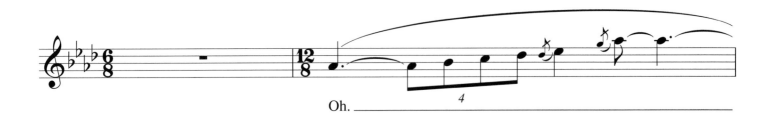

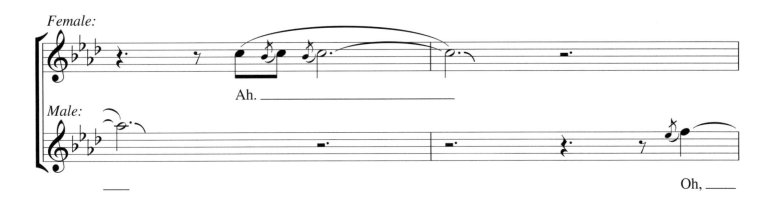

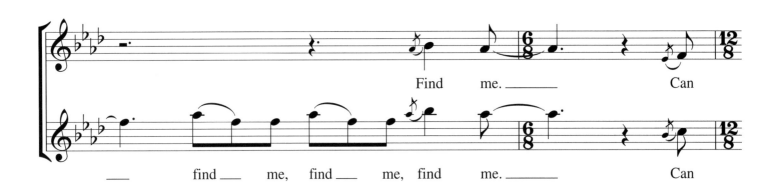

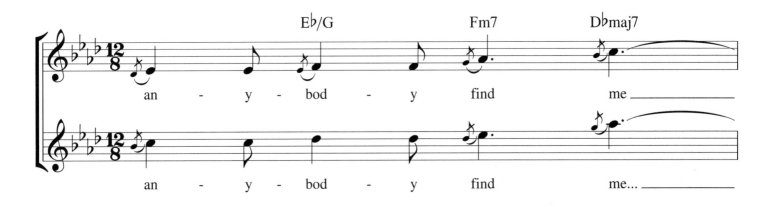

96

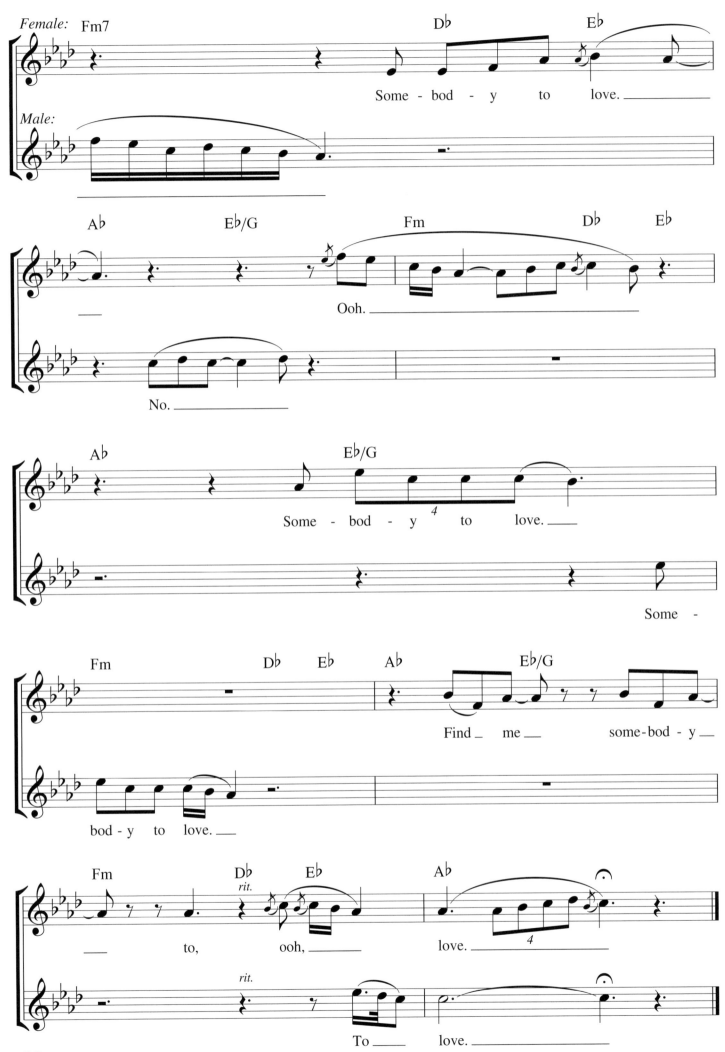

98

Sweet Caroline

Words and Music by Neil Diamond

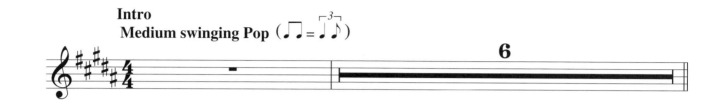

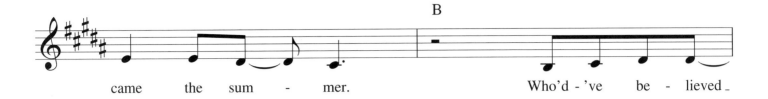

came the sum - mer.   Who'd - 've be - lieved _

____ you'd _ come a - long? ____

Pre-Chorus

Hands _____   touch - ing hands, _____

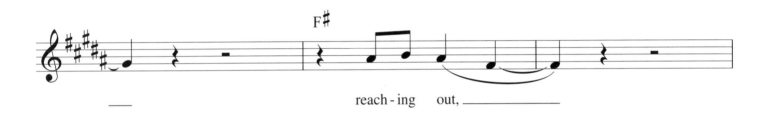

____   reach - ing out, _____

touch - ing me,   touch - ing you. _____

Chorus

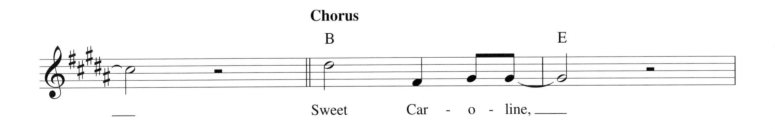

____   Sweet Car - o - line, ____

good times nev - er seemed _ so _____ good.

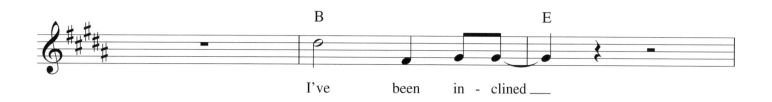

I've been in - clined ___

to be - lieve ___ they nev - er would. ___

Verse

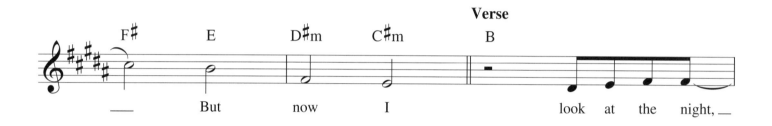

___ But now I look at the night, ___

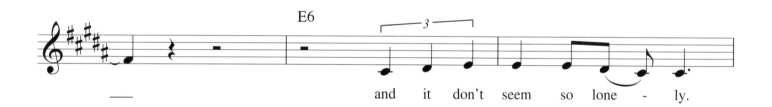

___ and it don't seem so lone - ly.

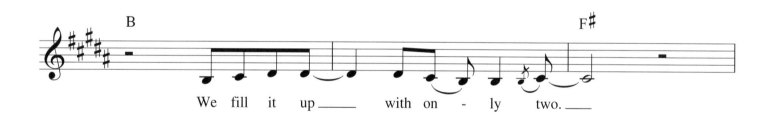

We fill it up ___ with on - ly two. ___

And when I hurt, ___

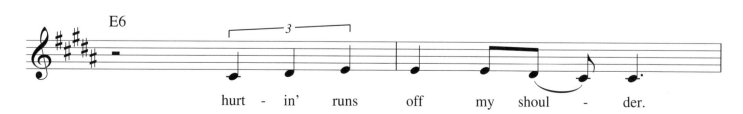

hurt - in' runs off my shoul - der.

How can I hurt _____ when ___ hold - ing ___

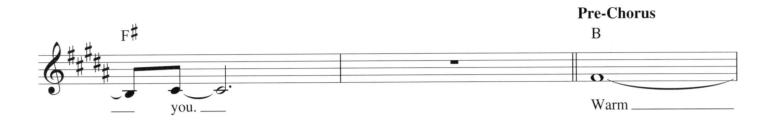
Pre-Chorus
___ you. ___ Warm ___

___ touch - ing warm, ___

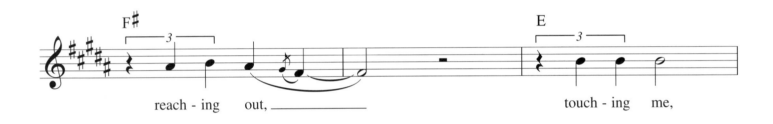
reach - ing out, ___ touch - ing me,

touch - ing you. ___

Chorus
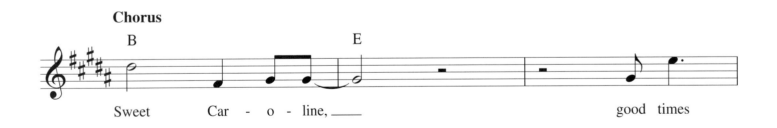
Sweet Car - o - line, ___ good times

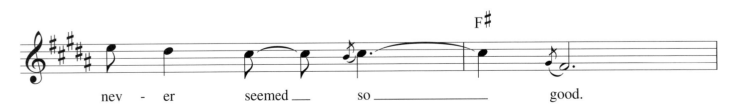
nev - er seemed ___ so ___ good.

I've   been   in - clined ___

to   be - lieve ___   they   nev - er   would, ___   oh,

Interlude

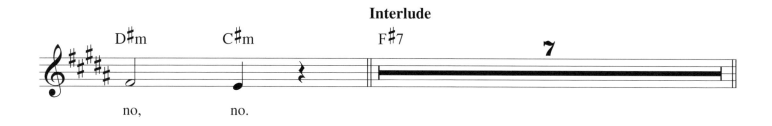

no,   no.

Chorus

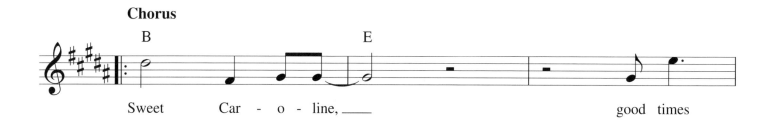

Sweet   Car - o - line, ___   good   times

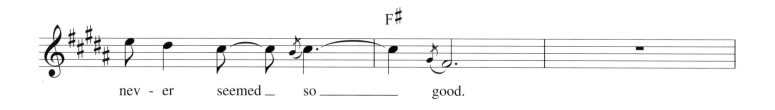

nev - er   seemed ___   so ___   good.

Sweet   Car - o - line, ___   I   be - lieved ___
I've   been   in - clined ___   to   be - lieve ___

Repeat and Fade

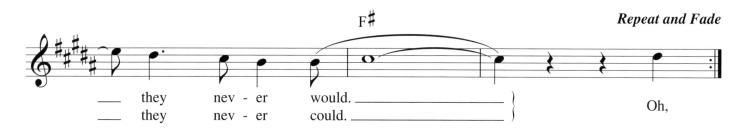

___ they   nev - er   would. ___
___ they   nev - er   could. ___   Oh,

Stand by Me

**Words and Music by Jerry Leiber,
Mike Stoller and Ben E. King**

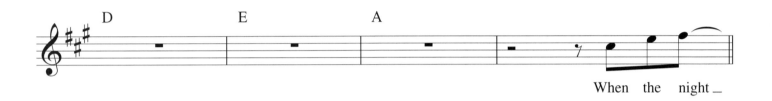

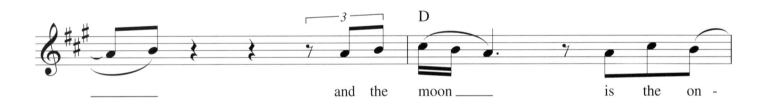

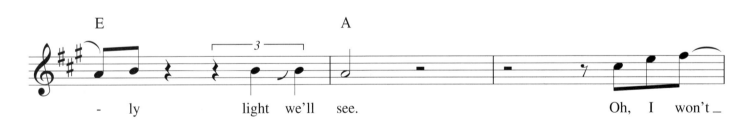

Chorus

Interlude

Verse

106

Stayin' Alive

from the Motion Picture SATURDAY NIGHT FEVER
Words and Music by Barry Gibb, Robin Gibb and Maurice Gibb

Oh, __ when you walk. _____   2. Well now,   I __

Verse

__ get __ low, and I _____ get high, __ and if I

can't get ei - ther,   I real - ly try.   Got the

wings of heav - en on __ my shoes. __ I'm a danc -

D.S. al Coda 1

- in' man,   and I just __ can't   lose. __ You know it's

Coda 1

__   Ah. _____

Bridge

Life go - in' no - where. _____   Some - bod - y help   me. _____

Some - bod - y help __ me, yeah. _____

110

Life go - in' no - where. _____ Some - bod - y help _ me, yeah. _

D.S.S. al Coda 2

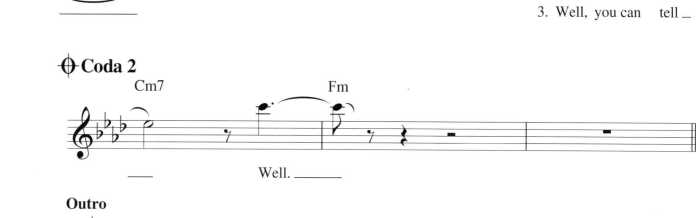

3. Well, you can tell _

⊕ Coda 2

_ Well. _____

Outro

Life go - in' no - where. _____ Some-bod - y help me. _____

Some - bod - y help _ me, yeah. _____

Life go - in' no - where. _____

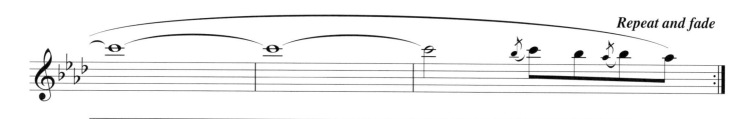

Some - bod - y help _ me, yeah. _____ I'm stay-in' a - live. _

Repeat and fade

Summer of '69

Words and Music by Bryan Adams and Jim Vallance

six - ty - nine. ___   Oh. ___

Bridge

Man, ___ we were kill - in' time. ___ We were ___ young and rest - less, we

need - ed to un - wind.   I guess noth - in' can last ___ for - ev -

Interlude

- er, for - ev - er. ___ No!

Yeah.

D   A

Verse

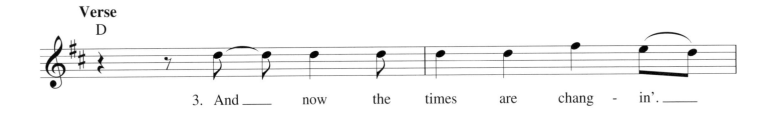

3. And ___ now the times are chang - in'. ___

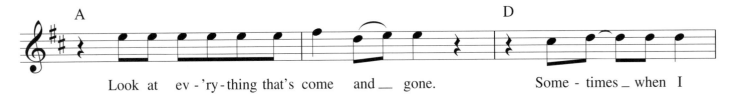

Look at ev - 'ry-thing that's come and ___ gone.   Some - times ___ when I

114

play that old six - string, __ think a - bout ya, won - der what went wrong.

 Coda 2
Outro-Chorus

life. Oh, __ yeah. __ Back in the sum - mer of

six - ty - nine. __ Uh, huh. __ It was the sum - mer of

six - ty - nine. _____ Oh, __ yeah. __ Me and my ba - by in

six - ty - nine. __ Oh. _____ Whoa.

It was the sum - mer, the sum - mer, the sum - mer of

six - ty - nine. __ Yeah. __

Repeat and fade

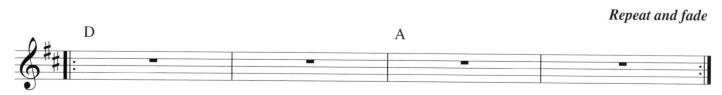

That'll Be the Day

Words and Music by Jerry Allison, Norman Petty and Buddy Holly

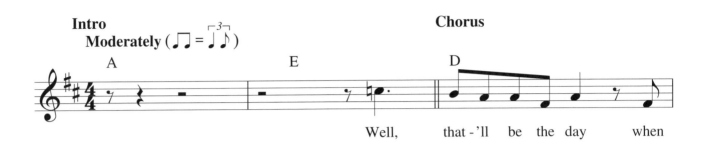

Well, that-'ll be the day when

you say, "Good-bye." Yes, __ that-'ll be the day when you make me cry. __ You

say you're gon-na leave, you know it's a lie __ 'cause that-'ll be the day __

__ when I die. __ 1. Well, you give me all your lov-in' and your tur-tle-dov-in', a-

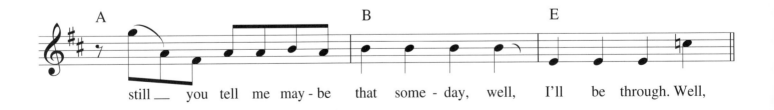

all your hugs and kiss-es and your mon-ey, too. __ Well, __ uh you know you love me, ba-by,

still __ you tell me may-be that some-day, well, I'll be through. Well,

that-'ll be the day when you say, "Good-bye." Yes, _____ that-'ll be the day when

you make my cry. _ You say you're gon-na leave, you know it's a lie __ 'cause _

Interlude

10

that-'ll be the day _____ when I die. _

Chorus

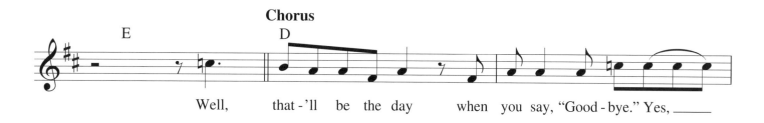

Well, that-'ll be the day when you say, "Good-bye." Yes, _____

that-'ll be the day when you make me cry. _ You say you're gon-na leave, you

know it's a lie __ 'cause that-'ll be the day _____ when I die. _ 2. Well,

Verse

when Cu-pid shot his dart, _ he shot it at your heart. _ So if we ev-er part, _ then

I'll leave you. You say, "then hold me," and you tell — me bold-ly that —

Chorus

— some-day, well, I'll be through. Well, that-'ll be the day when

you say, "Good-bye." Yes, _____ that-'ll be the day when you make me cry. — You

say you're gon-na leave, you know it's a lie _____ 'cause that-'ll be the day _____

Outro

_____ when I die. _____ Well, that-'ll be the day, ooh. _____

That-'ll be the day, ooh. _____ Uh, that-'ll be the day,

ooh. _____ Uh, that-'ll be the day.

That's Amoré
(That's Love)

from the Paramount Picture THE CADDY
Words by Jack Brooks
Music by Harry Warren

Rubato

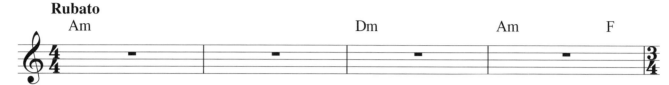

Moderately fast

When the moon hits your eye like a big piz - za

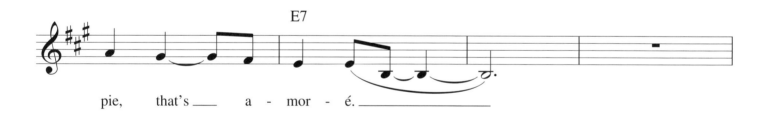

pie, that's ___ a - mor - é. ___

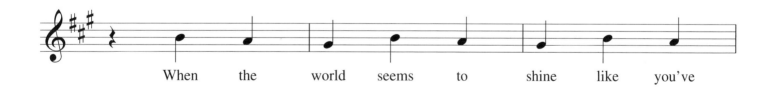

When the world seems to shine like you've

had too much ___ wine, ___ that's ___ a - mor - é. ___

Bells will ring, ting - a - ling - a -

ling, ting - a - ling - a - ling, and you'll sing, "Vi - ta

Bel - la." _____ Hearts will

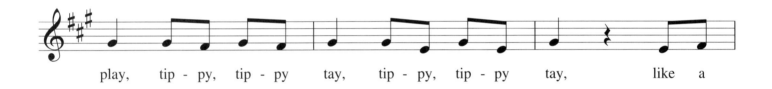

play, tip - py, tip - py tay, tip - py, tip - py tay, like a

gay tar - an - tel - la. _____

When the stars make you drool just like pas - ta fa -

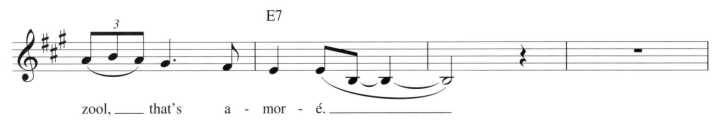

zool, ___ that's a - mor - é. _____

When you dance down the street with a cloud at your

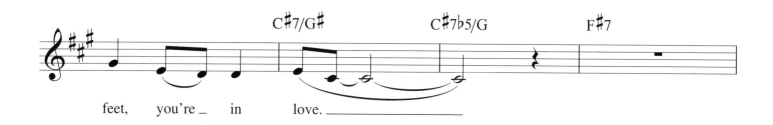

feet, you're in love.

When you walk in a dream, but you know you're not

dream - ing, Si - gno - ré.

Scuz - za me, but you see back in ol' Nap - o -

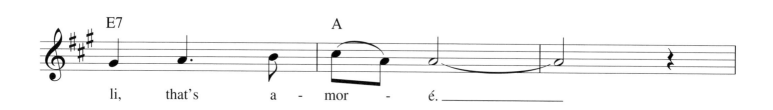

li, that's a - mor - é.

That's _ a - mor - é. _____

That's _ a - mor - é. _____

Luck - y fel - la. _____ When

the stars make you drool just like pas - ta fa -

zool, that's ___ a - mor - é. _____

When you dance down the street with a cloud at your

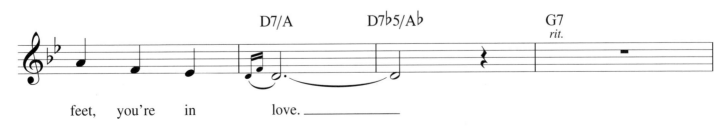

feet, you're in love. _____

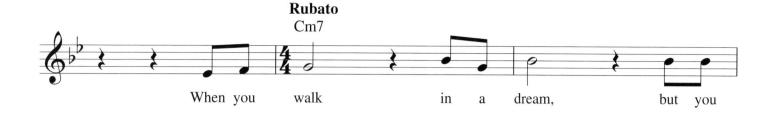

Rubato

When you walk in a dream, but you

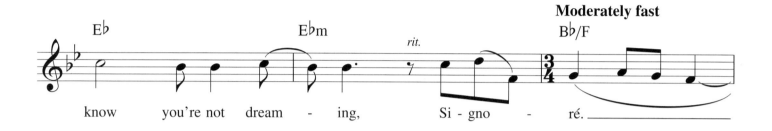

know you're not dream - ing, Si - gno - ré. _____

Moderately fast

_____ Scuz - za me, but you

see back in ol' Nap - o - li, that's a - mor - é. _____

That's _____ a -

mor - é. _____

123

Ticket to Ride

Words and Music by John Lennon and Paul McCartney

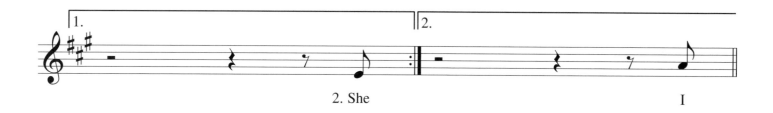

1.

2.

2. She

I

Bridge

D7

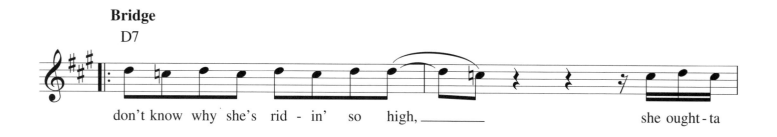

don't know why she's rid - in' so high, _____ she ought - ta

E

think twice, she ought - ta do right by me. Be -

D7

fore she gets to say - in' good - bye, _____ she ought - ta

E

think twice, she ought - ta do right by me.

Verse

A

3. I think I'm gon - na be sad, _____ I think it's to - day, ___
4. She says that liv - in' with me _____ is bring - in' her down, _

_____ yeah.
_____ yeah.

The girl that's driv-in' me mad____
She would nev-er be free____

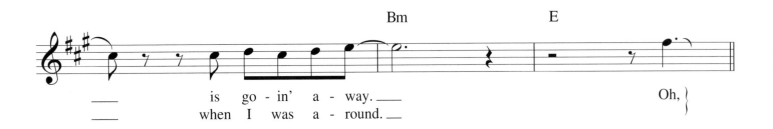

Bm   E

____ is go-in' a - way.____
____ when I was a - round.____

Oh,

Chorus

F#m   D7   F#m

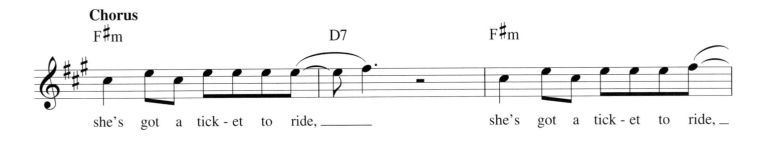

she's got a tick-et to ride, _____   she's got a tick-et to ride, ___

Gmaj7   F#m   E

_____   she's got a tick-et to ride, ___   but she don't care. ___

A

1.   **2.**

____   I   My ba - by don't

Outro   *Repeat and fade*

A

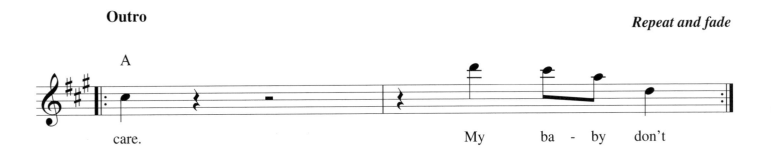

care.   My ba - by don't

You Are the Sunshine of My Life

Words and Music by Stevie Wonder

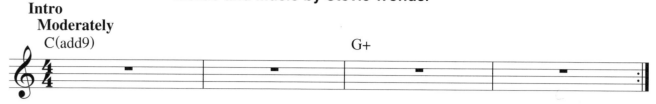

Intro
Moderately

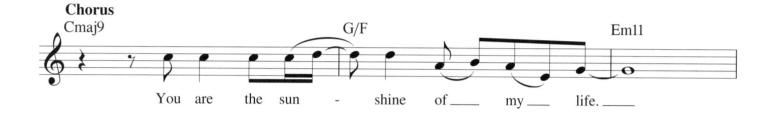

Chorus

You are the sun - shine of my life.

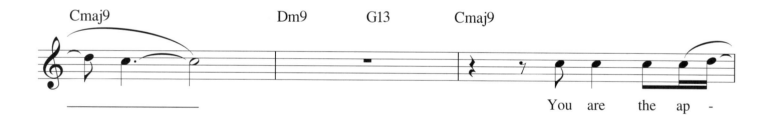

That's why I'll al - ways be a - round.

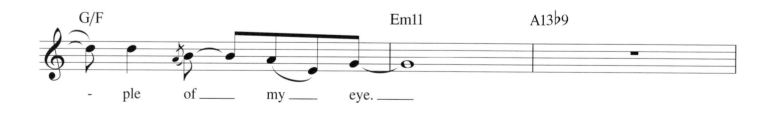

You are the ap -

- ple of my eye.

For - ev - er you'll stay in my heart.

You Raise Me Up

Words and Music by Brendan Graham and Rolf Lovland

up to walk ___ on storm - y seas. _____ I am

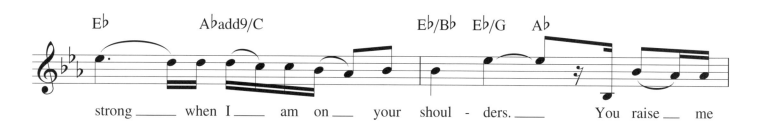

strong _____ when I ____ am on ___ your shoul - ders. _____ You raise ___ me

up to more ___ than I ____ can ___ be.

Interlude

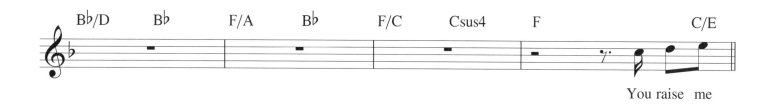

You raise me

Chorus

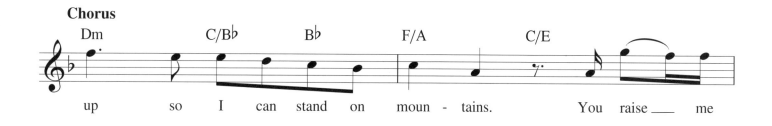

up so I can stand on moun - tains. You raise ___ me

up to walk ___ on storm - y seas. I _____ am ___

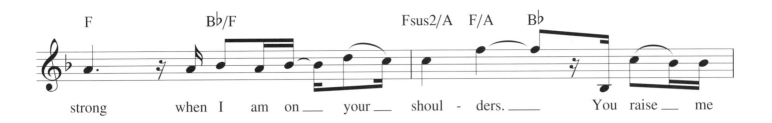

strong when I am on your shoul - ders. You raise me

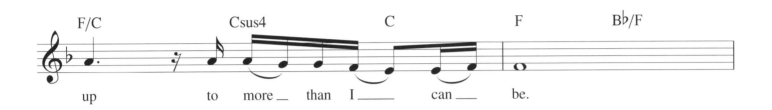

up to more than I can be.

Chorus

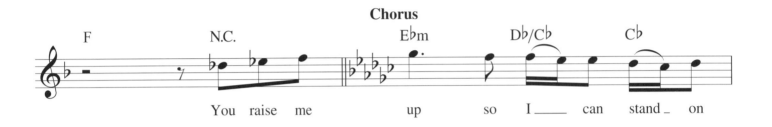

You raise me up so I can stand on

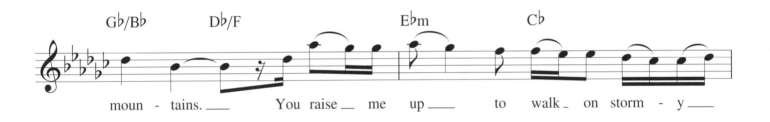

moun - tains. You raise me up to walk on storm - y

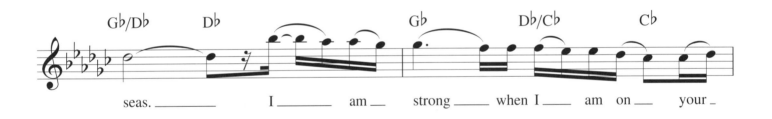

seas. I am strong when I am on your

shoul - ders. You raise me up to more than I can

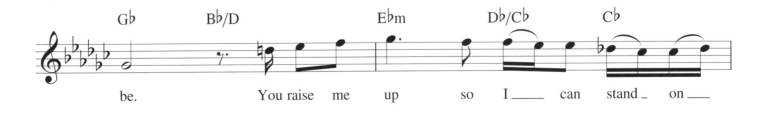

be. You raise me up so I can stand on

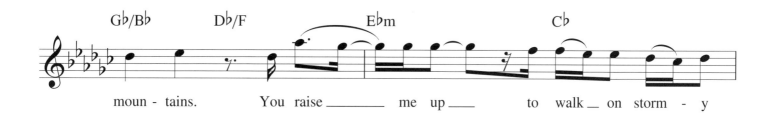

moun - tains. You raise ____ me up __ to walk _ on storm - y

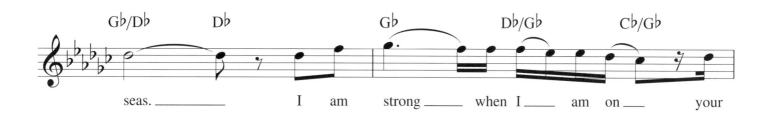

seas. _____ I am strong ____ when I ___ am on __ your

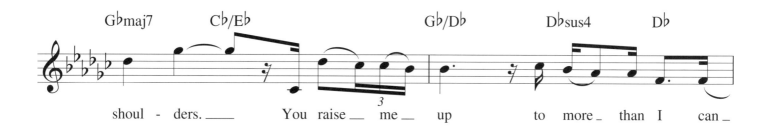

shoul - ders. ___ You raise _ me _ up to more _ than I can _

_ be. _____ You raise me ___

up to more ___ than _ I _____

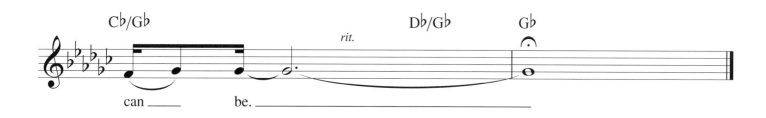

can ___ be. _____

You Give Love a Bad Name

Words and Music by Jon Bon Jovi, Desmond Child and Richie Sambora

Intro
Moderate Rock

Shot through the heart ___ and you're to ___ blame, dar - lin',

you give ___ love ___ a bad ___ name.

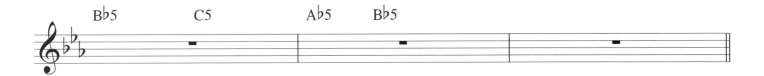

1. An

Verse

an - gel's smile ___ is what you sell, you prom-ised me heav - en and
2. See additional lyrics

put me through hell. ___ Chains of ___ love ___ got a

Additional Lyrics

2. You paint your smile on your lips.
   Blood-red nails on your fingertips.
   A school boy's dream, you act so shy.
   Your very first kiss was your first kiss goodbye.

BETTER THAN KARAOKE!

Pro Vocal® Series
SONGBOOK & SOUND-ALIKE CD
SING 8 GREAT SONGS
WITH A PROFESSIONAL BAND

Whether you're a karaoke singer or an auditioning professional, the Pro Vocal® series is for you! Unlike most karaoke packs, each book in the Pro Vocal Series contains the lyrics, melody, and chord symbols for eight hit songs. The CD contains demos for listening, and separate backing tracks so you can sing along. The CD is playable on any CD player, but it is also enhanced so PC and Mac computer users can adjust the recording to any pitch without changing the tempo! Perfect for home rehearsal, parties, auditions, corporate events, and gigs without a backup band.

WOMEN'S EDITIONS

00740247	1. Broadway Songs	$14.95
00740249	2. Jazz Standards	$14.95
00740246	3. Contemporary Hits	$14.95
00740277	4. '80s Gold	$12.95
00740299	5. Christmas Standards	$15.95
00740281	6. Disco Fever	$12.95
00740279	7. R&B Super Hits	$12.95
00740309	8. Wedding Gems	$12.95
00740409	9. Broadway Standards	$14.95
00740348	10. Andrew Lloyd Webber	$14.95
00740344	11. Disney's Best	$14.99
00740378	12. Ella Fitzgerald	$14.95
00740350	14. Musicals of Boublil & Schönberg	$14.95
00740377	15. Kelly Clarkson	$14.95
00740342	16. Disney Favorites	$14.99
00740353	17. Jazz Ballads	$14.99
00740376	18. Jazz Vocal Standards	$14.95
00740375	20. Hannah Montana	$16.95
00740354	21. Jazz Favorites	$14.99
00740374	22. Patsy Cline	$14.95
00740369	23. Grease	$14.95
00740367	25. ABBA	$14.95
00740365	26. Movie Songs	$14.95
00740360	28. High School Musical 1 & 2	$14.95
00740363	29. Torch Songs	$14.95
00740379	30. Hairspray	$14.95
00740380	31. Top Hits	$14.95
00740384	32. Hits of the '70s	$14.95
00740388	33. Billie Holiday	$14.95
00740389	34. The Sound of Music	$15.99
00740390	35. Contemporary Christian	$14.95
00740392	36. Wicked	$15.99
00740393	37. More Hannah Montana	$14.95
00740394	38. Miley Cyrus	$14.95
00740396	39. Christmas Hits	$15.95
00740410	40. Broadway Classics	$14.95
00740415	41. Broadway Favorites	$14.99
00740416	42. Great Standards You Can Sing	$14.99
00740417	43. Singable Standards	$14.99
00740418	44. Favorite Standards	$14.99
00740419	45. Sing Broadway	$14.99
00740420	46. More Standards	$14.99
00740421	47. Timeless Hits	$14.99
00740422	48. Easygoing R&B	$14.99
00740424	49. Taylor Swift	$14.99
00740425	50. From This Moment On	$14.99
00740426	51. Great Standards Collection	$19.99
00740430	52. Worship Favorites	$14.99
00740434	53. Lullabyes	$14.99
00740438	54. Lady Gaga	$14.99

MEN'S EDITIONS

00740248	1. Broadway Songs	$14.95
00740250	2. Jazz Standards	$14.95
00740251	3. Contemporary Hits	$14.99
00740278	4. '80s Gold	$12.95
00740298	5. Christmas Standards	$15.95
00740280	6. R&B Super Hits	$12.95
00740282	7. Disco Fever	$12.95
00740310	8. Wedding Gems	$12.95
00740411	9. Broadway Greats	$14.99
00740333	10. Elvis Presley – Volume 1	$14.95
00740349	11. Andrew Lloyd Webber	$14.95
00740345	12. Disney's Best	$14.95
00740347	13. Frank Sinatra Classics	$14.95
00740334	14. Lennon & McCartney	$14.99
00740335	16. Elvis Presley – Volume 2	$14.99
00740343	17. Disney Favorites	$14.95
00740351	18. Musicals of Boublil & Schönberg	$14.95
00740346	20. Frank Sinatra Standards	$14.95
00740358	22. Great Standards	$14.99
00740341	24. Duke Ellington	$14.99
00740359	26. Pop Standards	$14.99
00740362	27. Michael Bublé	$14.95
00740361	28. High School Musical 1 & 2	$14.95
00740364	29. Torch Songs	$14.95
00740366	30. Movie Songs	$14.95
00740368	31. Hip Hop Hits	$14.95
00740370	32. Grease	$14.95
00740371	33. Josh Groban	$14.95
00740373	34. Billy Joel	$14.99
00740381	35. Hits of the '50s	$14.95
00740382	36. Hits of the '60s	$14.95
00740383	37. Hits of the '70s	$14.95
00740385	38. Motown	$14.95
00740386	39. Hank Williams	$14.95
00740387	40. Neil Diamond	$14.95
00740391	41. Contemporary Christian	$14.95
00740397	42. Christmas Hits	$15.95
00740399	43. Ray	$14.95
00740400	44. The Rat Pack Hits	$14.99
00740401	45. Songs in the Style of Nat "King" Cole	$14.99
00740402	46. At the Lounge	$14.95
00740403	47. The Big Band Singer	$14.95
00740404	48. Jazz Cabaret Songs	$14.99
00740405	49. Cabaret Songs	$14.99
00740406	50. Big Band Standards	$14.99
00740412	51. Broadway's Best	$14.99
00740427	52. Great Standards Collection	$19.99
00740431	53. Worship Favorites	$14.99
00740435	54. Barry Manilow	$14.99
00740436	55. Lionel Richie	$14.99

MIXED EDITIONS

These editions feature songs for both male and female voices.

00740311	1. Wedding Duets	$12.95
00740398	2. Enchanted	$14.95
00740407	3. Rent	$14.95
00740408	4. Broadway Favorites	$14.99
00740413	5. South Pacific	$15.99
00740414	6. High School Musical 3	$14.99
00740429	7. Christmas Carols	$14.99
00740437	8. Glee	$14.99

FOR MORE INFORMATION, SEE YOUR LOCAL MUSIC DEALER, OR WRITE TO:

HAL•LEONARD® CORPORATION

7777 W. BLUEMOUND RD. P.O. BOX 13819 MILWAUKEE, WI 53213

Visit Hal Leonard online at www.halleonard.com

Prices, contents, & availability subject to change without notice.
Disney charaters and artwork © Disney Enterprises, Inc.

0910

SING WITH THE CHOIR

CD INCLUDED

These **GREAT COLLECTIONS** let singers
BECOME PART OF A FULL CHOIR and sing along
with some of the most-loved songs of all time.

Each book includes SATB parts (arrangements are enlarged from octavo-size to 9" x 12")
and the accompanying CD features full, professionally recorded performances.

Now you just need to turn on the CD, open the book, pick your part, and
SING ALONG WITH THE CHOIR!

1. ANDREW LLOYD WEBBER
Any Dream Will Do • As If We Never Said Goodbye • Don't Cry for Me Argentina • Love Changes Everything • Memory • The Music of the Night • Pie Jesu • Whistle down the Wind.
00333001 Book/CD Pack.............................. $14.95

2. BROADWAY
Bring Him Home • Cabaret • For Good • Luck Be a Lady • Seasons of Love • There's No Business like Show Business • Where Is Love? • You'll Never Walk Alone.
00333002 Book/CD Pack.............................. $14.95

3. STANDARDS
Cheek to Cheek • Georgia on My Mind • I Left My Heart in San Francisco • I'm Beginning to See the Light • Moon River • On the Sunny Side of the Street • Skylark • When I Fall in Love.
00333003 Book/CD Pack.............................. $14.95

4. THE 1950s
At the Hop • The Great Pretender • Kansas City • La Bamba • Love Me Tender • My Prayer • Rock Around the Clock • Unchained Melody.
00333004 Book/CD Pack.............................. $14.95

5. THE 1960s
All You Need is Love • Can't Help Falling in Love • Dancing in the Street • Good Vibrations • I Heard It Through the Grapevine • I'm a Believer • Under the Boardwalk • What a Wonderful World.
00333005 Book/CD Pack.............................. $14.95

6. THE 1970s
Ain't No Mountain High Enough • Bohemian Rhapsody • I'll Be There • Imagine • Let It Be • Night Fever • Yesterday Once More • You Are the Sunshine of My Life.
00333006 Book/CD Pack.............................. $14.95

7. DISNEY FAVORITES
The Bare Necessities • Be Our Guest • Circle of Life • Cruella De Vil • Friend like Me • Hakuna Matata • Joyful, Joyful • Under the Sea.
00333007 Book/CD Pack.............................. $14.95

8. DISNEY HITS
Beauty and the Beast • Breaking Free • Can You Feel the Love Tonight • Candle on the Water • Colors of the Wind • A Whole New World (Aladdin's Theme) • You'll Be in My Heart • You've Got a Friend in Me.
00333008 Book/CD Pack.............................. $14.95

9. LES MISÉRABLES
At the End of the Day • Bring Him Home • Castle on a Cloud • Do You Hear the People Sing? • Finale • I Dreamed a Dream • On My Own • One Day More.
00333009 Book/CD Pack.............................. $14.99

10. CHRISTMAS FAVORITES
Frosty the Snow Man • The Holiday Season • (There's No Place Like) Home for the Holidays • Little Saint Nick • Merry Christmas, Darling • Santa Claus Is Comin' to Town • Silver Bells • White Christmas.
00333011 Book/CD Pack.............................. $14.95

11. CHRISTMAS TIME IS HERE
Blue Christmas • Christmas Time is Here • Feliz Navidad • Happy Xmas (War Is Over) • I'll Be Home for Christmas • Let It Snow! Let It Snow! Let It Snow! • We Need a Little Christmas • Wonderful Christmastime.
00333012 Book/CD Pack.............................. $14.95

12. THE SOUND OF MUSIC
Climb Ev'ry Mountain • Do-Re-Mi • Edelweiss • The Lonely Goatherd • My Favorite Things • So Long, Farewell • The Sound of Music.
00333019 Book/CD Pack.............................. $14.99

13. CHRISTMAS CAROLS
Angels We Have Heard on High • Deck the Hall • Go, Tell It on the Mountain • Joy to the World • O Come, All Ye Faithful (Adeste Fideles) • O Holy Night • Silent Night • We Wish You a Merry Christmas.
00333020 Book/CD Pack.............................. $14.99

14. GLEE
Can't Fight This Feeling • Don't Stop Believin' • Jump • Keep Holding On • Lean on Me • No Air • Rehab • Somebody to Love.
00333059 Book/CD Pack.............................. $16.99

FOR MORE INFORMATION, SEE YOUR LOCAL MUSIC DEALER,
OR WRITE TO:

HAL•LEONARD®
C O R P O R A T I O N
7777 W. BLUEMOUND RD. P.O. BOX 13819 MILWAUKEE, WI 53213

Prices, contents, and availability
subject to change without notice.

0410

ORIGINAL KEYS FOR SINGERS

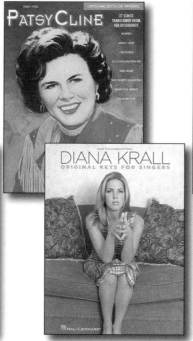

ACROSS THE UNIVERSE

Authentic vocal/piano transcriptions of 20 Beatles tunes from the Golden Globe and Oscar-nominated musical directed by Julie Taymor. Includes: Because • Blackbird • Hey Jude • Let It Be • Revolution • Something • and more.
00307010 Vocal Transcriptions with Piano $19.95

LOUIS ARMSTRONG

Features authentic vocal/piano transcriptions of 17 Satchmo classics in their original keys! Includes: Dream a Little Dream of Me • Hello, Dolly! • Mack the Knife • Makin' Whoopee! • Mame • St. Louis Blues • What a Wonderful World • Zip-A-Dee-Doo-Dah • and more.
00307029 Vocal Transcriptions with Piano $19.99

MARIAH CAREY

Vocal transcriptions of all five octaves of this pop diva's 20 most popular tunes, including: Always Be My Baby • Dreamlover • Emotions • Heartbreaker • Hero • I Don't Wanna Cry • Love Takes Time • Loverboy • One Sweet Day • Vision of Love • We Belong Together • and more.
00306835 Vocal Transcriptions with Piano $19.95

PATSY CLINE

The definitive Patsy Cline book for singers! 27 top songs in the original key, newly transcribed from the original recordings. For voice with piano accompaniment, with chord symbols. Includes: Always • Blue Moon of Kentucky • Crazy • Faded Love • I Fall to Pieces • Just a Closer Walk with Thee • Sweet Dreams • more. Also includes a biography.
00740072 Vocal Transcriptions with Piano $14.95

FOR MORE INFORMATION,
SEE YOUR LOCAL MUSIC DEALER,
OR WRITE TO:

HAL•LEONARD®
CORPORATION
7777 W. BLUEMOUND RD. P.O. BOX 13819
MILWAUKEE, WISCONSIN 53213

www.halleonard.com

ELLA FITZGERALD

This fine book features authentic transcriptions in the original keys of 25 Fitzgerald classics in voice with piano accompaniment format: A-tisket, A-tasket • But Not for Me • Easy to Love • Embraceable You • The Lady Is a Tramp • Misty • Oh, Lady Be Good! • Satin Doll • Stompin' at the Savoy • Take the "A" Train • and more. Includes a biography and discography.
00740252 Vocal Transcriptions with Piano $16.95

JOSH GROBAN

Alejate • Awake • Believe • February Song • In Her Eyes • L'Ultima Notte • Lullaby • Machine • Mai • Never Let Go • Now or Never • O Holy Night • Per Te • The Prayer • Remember When It Rained • So She Dances • To Where You Are • Un Amore Per Sempre • Un Dia Llegara • You Are Loved (Don't Give Up) • You Raise Me Up • You're Still You.
00306969 Vocal Transcriptions with Piano $19.99

BILLIE HOLIDAY

TRANSCRIBED FROM HISTORIC RECORDINGS

This groundbreaking publication features authentic transcriptions in the original keys of 19 classics from the key signature recordings of the great Lady Day. Includes Billie's Blues (I Love My Man) • Body and Soul • Crazy He Calls Me • Easy Living • A Fine Romance • God Bless' the Child • Lover, Come Back to Me • Miss Brown to You • Strange Fruit • The Very Thought of You • and more.
00740140 Vocal Transcriptions with Piano $14.95

DIANA KRALL

20 of the signature songs of jazz vocalist/pianist Diana Krall. Includes: All or Nothing at All • The Frim Fram Sauce • The Girl in the Other Room • Hit That Jive Jack • The Look of Love • 'S Wonderful • This Can't Be Love • and more.
00306743 Vocal Transcriptions with Piano $19.95

NANCY LAMOTT

Cabaret singer Nancy LaMott died in 1995 at age 43, leaving behind five CDs filled with her signature songs arranged and played by her music director, Christopher Marlowe. 21 of these beloved renditions are available here: Autumn Leaves • Downtown • I Have Dreamed • It Might as Well Be Spring • Moon River • Skylark • That Old Black Magic • and more.
00306995 Vocal Transcriptions with Piano $19.99

LEONA LEWIS – SPIRIT

Now you can sing all 14 track's from Leona's smash hit album with this collection that features piano accompaniments and the vocal lines in the original keys. Songs include: Better in Time • Bleeding Love • The First Time Ever I Saw Your Face • Here I Am • Homeless • I Will Be • I'm You • Whatever It Takes • Yesterday • and more.
00307007 Vocal Transcriptions with Piano $17.95

THE BEST OF LIZA MINNELLI

25 signature standards, all transcribed exactly as recorded, in their original keys! Includes: And All That Jazz • Cabaret • Losing My Mind • Maybe This Time • Me and My Baby • Theme from "New York, New York" • Ring Them Bells • Sara Lee • Say Liza (Liza with a Z) • Shine It On • Sing Happy • The Singer • Taking a Chance on Love.
00306928 Vocal Transcriptions with Piano $19.99

THE VERY BEST OF FRANK SINATRA

40 swingin' Sinatra classic tunes arranged in their original keys. Includes: Come Fly with Me • I've Got You Under My Skin • It Was a Very Good Year • My Way • Night and Day • Summer Wind • The Way You Look Tonight • You Make Me Feel So Young • and more. Includes biography.
00306753 Vocal Transcriptions with Piano $19.95

STEVE TYRELL – BACK TO BACHARACH

Our matching folio to Steve Tyrell's tribute to Burt Bacharach features the actual vocal transcriptions of 14 classics, including: Alfie • Always Something There to Remind Me • Close to You • I Say a Little Prayer • The Look of Love • Raindrops Keep Fallin' on My Head • This Guy's in Love with You • Walk on By • and more.
00307024 Vocal Transcriptions with Piano $16.99

SARAH VAUGHAN

The *All Music Guide* calls Vaughan "one of the most wondrous voices of the 20th century." This collection gathers 25 of her classics arranged in her original keys so today's singers can try to match her performances. Songs include: Black Coffee • If You Could See Me Now • It Might as Well Be Spring • My Funny Valentine • The Nearness of You • A Night in Tunisia • Perdido • September Song • Tenderly • and more.
00306558 Vocal Transcriptions with Piano $17.95

Audition Songs

Ace your audition with these great collections from MUSIC SALES AMERICA!

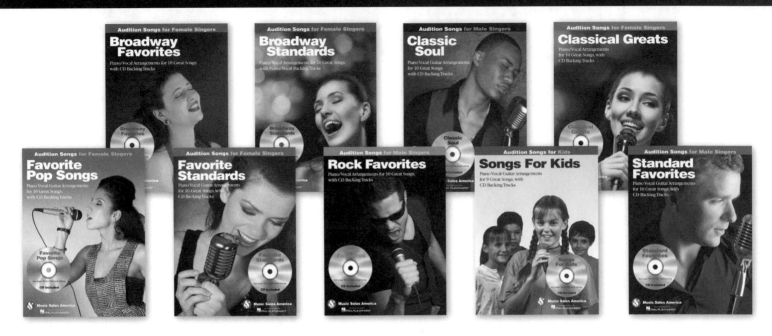

No more problems finding an accompanist!
Make a big impression with these books each featuring 10 great songs, carefully selected for singers auditioning for shows or bands.

Broadway Favorites – Female Singers
As If We Never Said Goodbye • Cabaret • Don't Cry for Me Argentina • I Don't Know How to Love Him • I Dreamed a Dream • If My Friends Could See Me Now • Memory • My Favorite Things • What I Did for Love • The Winner Takes It All.
14031159 P/V/G $14.99

Broadway Favorites – Male Singers
Anthem • Bring Him Home • If I Loved You • Luck Be a Lady • Maria • Some Enchanted Evening • This Is the Moment • Tonight • What Kind of Fool Am I? • Why God Why?
14033430 P/V/G $14.99

Broadway Standards – Female Singers
Another Suitcase in Another Hall • As Long As He Needs Me • Big Spender • Can't Help Lovin' Dat Man • Feeling Good • I Cain't Say No • If I Were a Bell • On My Own • Take That Look off Your Face • Wishing You Were Somehow Here Again.
14033410 P/V/G $14.99

Classic Soul – Male Singers
Drift Away • Everybody Needs Somebody to Love • Hold on I'm Comin' • I Get the Sweetest Feeling • I Got You (I Feel Good) • In the Midnight Hour • Love Really Hurts Without You • (Sittin' On) The Dock of the Bay • Tired of Being Alone • Unchain My Heart.
14037455 P/V/G $14.99

Classical Greats – Female Singers
Caro mio ben • Caro Nome • Habanera • Panis Angelicus (O Lord Most Holy) • Voi, Che Sapete • When I Am Laid in Earth • Widmung.
14037457 P/V/G $14.99

Classical Greats – Male Singers
Ave Maria • Che Faro Senza Euridice? • Deh vieni alla finestra (Serenade) • Flower Song • It Was a Lover and His Lass • La donna e mobile • Una Furtiva Lagrima • Wiegenlied (Lullaby).
14037456 P/V/G $14.99

Favorite Pop Songs – Female Singers
Come What May • Don't Speak • From a Distance • Hero • I Will Always Love You • I Will Survive • Saving All My Love for You • That Don't Impress Me Much • The Wind Beneath My Wings • You Must Love Me.
14028738 P/V/G $14.99

Favorite Standards – Female Singers
Black Coffee • Crazy • Cry Me a River • Diamonds Are a Girl's Best Friend • God Bless' the Child • Lover Man (Oh, Where Can You Be?) • Moonglow • Smoke Gets in Your Eyes • Solitude • Someone to Watch over Me.
14031133 P/V/G $14.99

Rock Favorites – Male Singers
Dream On • Fields of Gold • Have I Told You Lately • The Joker • Light My Fire • A Little Less Conversation • Saturday Night's Alright (For Fighting) • Stuck in the Middle with You • Where the Streets Have No Name • Woman.
14036220 P/V/G $14.99

Songs for Kids
Any Dream Will Do • The Candy Man • Consider Yourself • Food, Glorious Food • Happy Talk • I'd Do Anything • Maybe • Thank You for the Music • Tomorrow.
14037458 P/V/G $14.99

Standard Favorites – Male Singers
Come Fly with Me • Fly Me to the Moon (In Other Words) • The Girl from Ipanema (Garôta De Ipanema) • The Lady Is a Tramp • Moon River • My Way • Strangers in the Night • (Love Is) The Tender Trap • That's Amoré (That's Love) • The Way You Look Tonight.
14037454 P/V/G $14.99

 Music Sales America

EXCLUSIVELY DISTRIBUTED BY
 **HAL•LEONARD**®

For more information, see your local music dealer, or visit www.halleonard.com

Prices, content, and availability subject to change without notice.